50 South Korean Cake Flavor Recipes for Home

By: Kelly Johnson

Table of Contents

- Red Bean Cake
- Matcha Green Tea Cake
- Sweet Potato Cake
- Black Sesame Cake
- Chestnut Cake
- Yogurt Cake
- Honey Cake
- Citron Cake
- Peach Cake
- Rice Cake (tteok)
- Kimchi Cake
- Green Tea and Red Bean Cake
- Pumpkin Cake
- Strawberry Cream Cake
- Mango Cake
- Choco-Chip Cake
- Jujube Cake
- Cinnamon Cake
- Almond Cake
- Spicy Rice Cake Cake
- Coconut Cake
- Lemon Cake
- Maple Cake
- Vanilla Cream Cake
- Ginger Cake
- Black Bean Cake
- Sesame and Honey Cake
- Lychee Cake
- Blueberry Cake
- Taro Cake
- Dalgona Coffee Cake
- Apple Cinnamon Cake
- Raspberry Cake
- Walnut Cake
- Pear Cake
- Chocolate Green Tea Cake

- Sweet Red Bean Paste Cake
- Carrot Cake
- Milk Cake
- Soybean Cake
- Cherry Blossom Cake
- Fig Cake
- Hazelnut Cake
- Apricot Cake
- Pineapple Cake
- Cocoa Cake
- Grape Cake
- Mochi Cake
- Sorghum Cake
- Chestnut and Red Bean Cake

Red Bean Cake

Ingredients:

For the Cake:

- 1 cup adzuki beans
- 1 cup sugar
- 1/2 cup water
- 1 1/2 cups cake flour
- 1 tsp baking powder
- 1/2 tsp salt
- 1/2 cup milk
- 1/2 cup vegetable oil
- 2 large eggs
- 1 tsp vanilla extract

For the Red Bean Filling:

- 1 cup cooked adzuki beans
- 1/2 cup sugar
- 1/4 cup water

Optional Toppings:

- Whipped cream
- Fresh fruit
- Sweetened condensed milk

Instructions:

1. **Prepare the Red Bean Filling:**
    - In a saucepan, combine the cooked adzuki beans, sugar, and water. Cook over medium heat until the mixture thickens, stirring frequently. Let it cool.
2. **Preheat Oven:**
    - Preheat your oven to 350°F (175°C). Grease and flour an 8-inch round cake pan.
3. **Make the Cake Batter:**
    - In a medium bowl, whisk together the cake flour, baking powder, and salt.
    - In a separate bowl, beat the eggs and sugar until light and fluffy. Add the milk, vegetable oil, and vanilla extract, and mix well.
    - Gradually add the dry ingredients to the wet mixture, mixing until just combined.
4. **Bake the Cake:**
    - Pour half of the cake batter into the prepared cake pan. Spoon the red bean filling evenly over the batter, then top with the remaining batter.
    - Bake in the preheated oven for 30-35 minutes, or until a toothpick inserted into the center comes out clean.

5. **Cool and Serve:**
    - Allow the cake to cool in the pan for 10 minutes before transferring it to a wire rack to cool completely.
    - Optional: Top with whipped cream, fresh fruit, or a drizzle of sweetened condensed milk before serving.

Enjoy your homemade Red Bean Cake!

Matcha Green Tea Cake

Ingredients:

For the Cake:

- 1 1/2 cups all-purpose flour
- 1 cup granulated sugar
- 1/2 cup unsalted butter, room temperature
- 2 large eggs
- 1/2 cup milk
- 1/4 cup plain yogurt (or sour cream)
- 2 tbsp matcha green tea powder
- 1 1/2 tsp baking powder
- 1/2 tsp baking soda
- 1/4 tsp salt
- 1 tsp vanilla extract

For the Frosting:

- 1 cup unsalted butter, room temperature
- 2 1/2 cups powdered sugar
- 2 tbsp matcha green tea powder
- 2-3 tbsp heavy cream or milk
- 1 tsp vanilla extract

Optional Garnish:

- Additional matcha powder
- Fresh fruit
- Edible flowers

Instructions:

1. **Preheat Oven:**
    - Preheat your oven to 350°F (175°C). Grease and flour an 8-inch round cake pan or line it with parchment paper.
2. **Prepare the Cake Batter:**
    - In a medium bowl, whisk together the flour, baking powder, baking soda, salt, and matcha green tea powder.
    - In a large bowl, cream the butter and sugar together until light and fluffy.
    - Add the eggs one at a time, beating well after each addition. Mix in the vanilla extract.
    - Gradually add the dry ingredients to the butter mixture, alternating with the milk and yogurt, beginning and ending with the dry ingredients. Mix until just combined.

3. **Bake the Cake:**
    - Pour the batter into the prepared cake pan and smooth the top.
    - Bake for 25-30 minutes, or until a toothpick inserted into the center comes out clean.
    - Let the cake cool in the pan for 10 minutes before transferring it to a wire rack to cool completely.
4. **Prepare the Frosting:**
    - In a large bowl, beat the butter until creamy. Gradually add the powdered sugar, matcha powder, and vanilla extract, mixing until smooth.
    - Add heavy cream or milk, one tablespoon at a time, until the frosting reaches your desired consistency.
5. **Frost the Cake:**
    - Once the cake is completely cool, spread a layer of frosting on top. If you're using multiple layers, frost between the layers as well.
    - Smooth the frosting with a spatula or knife. Garnish with additional matcha powder, fresh fruit, or edible flowers if desired.
6. **Serve:**
    - Slice and enjoy your homemade Matcha Green Tea Cake!

This cake pairs beautifully with a cup of tea and makes for an elegant dessert.

Sweet Potato Cake

Ingredients:

For the Cake:

- 1 1/2 cups all-purpose flour
- 1 cup granulated sugar
- 1/2 cup brown sugar, packed
- 1/2 cup unsalted butter, room temperature
- 1 cup cooked and mashed sweet potatoes (about 1 medium sweet potato)
- 2 large eggs
- 1/2 cup milk
- 1/2 cup vegetable oil
- 1 tsp vanilla extract
- 1 tsp baking powder
- 1/2 tsp baking soda
- 1/2 tsp ground cinnamon
- 1/4 tsp ground nutmeg
- 1/4 tsp salt

For the Cream Cheese Frosting:

- 8 oz (225g) cream cheese, room temperature
- 1/2 cup unsalted butter, room temperature
- 3-4 cups powdered sugar
- 1 tsp vanilla extract

Optional Garnish:

- Chopped nuts (e.g., pecans or walnuts)
- Ground cinnamon
- Fresh herbs or edible flowers

Instructions:

1. **Prepare Sweet Potatoes:**
   - Preheat your oven to 400°F (200°C). Roast the sweet potato until tender (about 45-60 minutes). Let it cool, then peel and mash it. You need 1 cup of mashed sweet potato.
2. **Preheat Oven:**
   - Preheat your oven to 350°F (175°C). Grease and flour an 8-inch round cake pan or line it with parchment paper.
3. **Make the Cake Batter:**
   - In a medium bowl, whisk together the flour, baking powder, baking soda, cinnamon, nutmeg, and salt.

- In a large bowl, beat the butter, granulated sugar, and brown sugar until light and fluffy.
- Add the eggs one at a time, beating well after each addition. Mix in the vanilla extract.
- Add the mashed sweet potatoes and mix until well combined.
- Gradually add the dry ingredients to the wet ingredients, alternating with the milk and vegetable oil. Mix until just combined.

4. **Bake the Cake:**
    - Pour the batter into the prepared cake pan and smooth the top.
    - Bake for 30-35 minutes, or until a toothpick inserted into the center comes out clean.
    - Let the cake cool in the pan for 10 minutes before transferring it to a wire rack to cool completely.

5. **Prepare the Frosting:**
    - In a large bowl, beat the cream cheese and butter until creamy and smooth.
    - Gradually add the powdered sugar, beating until well combined and fluffy.
    - Mix in the vanilla extract.

6. **Frost the Cake:**
    - Once the cake is completely cool, spread the cream cheese frosting evenly over the cake.
    - Garnish with chopped nuts, a sprinkle of ground cinnamon, or fresh herbs if desired.

7. **Serve:**
    - Slice and enjoy your homemade Sweet Potato Cake!

This cake is a wonderful treat for any occasion and pairs beautifully with a cup of coffee or tea.

Black Sesame Cake

Ingredients:

For the Cake:

- 1 cup black sesame seeds
- 1 1/2 cups all-purpose flour
- 1 cup granulated sugar
- 1/2 cup unsalted butter, room temperature
- 2 large eggs
- 1/2 cup milk
- 1/2 cup plain yogurt (or sour cream)
- 1 1/2 tsp baking powder
- 1/2 tsp baking soda
- 1/4 tsp salt
- 1 tsp vanilla extract
- 1/4 cup vegetable oil

For the Black Sesame Filling (optional):

- 1/2 cup black sesame paste (store-bought or homemade)
- 1/4 cup granulated sugar

For the Frosting:

- 1 cup unsalted butter, room temperature
- 2 1/2 cups powdered sugar
- 2 tbsp black sesame seeds, finely ground
- 2-3 tbsp heavy cream or milk
- 1 tsp vanilla extract

Optional Garnish:

- Toasted black sesame seeds
- Fresh fruit or edible flowers

Instructions:

1. **Prepare the Black Sesame Seeds:**
   - Toast the black sesame seeds in a dry skillet over medium heat until fragrant and slightly darker (about 3-5 minutes). Let them cool.
   - Grind the toasted sesame seeds into a fine powder using a spice grinder or food processor.
2. **Preheat Oven:**

- Preheat your oven to 350°F (175°C). Grease and flour an 8-inch round cake pan or line it with parchment paper.

3. **Make the Cake Batter:**
    - In a medium bowl, whisk together the flour, baking powder, baking soda, and salt.
    - In a large bowl, cream the butter and sugar until light and fluffy.
    - Add the eggs one at a time, beating well after each addition. Mix in the vanilla extract.
    - Gradually add the black sesame powder to the butter mixture, mixing until combined.
    - Add the milk and yogurt alternately with the dry ingredients, beginning and ending with the dry ingredients. Mix until just combined.
    - Stir in the vegetable oil.
4. **Prepare the Black Sesame Filling (Optional):**
    - If using, mix the black sesame paste with granulated sugar in a small bowl until smooth.
5. **Bake the Cake:**
    - Pour half of the batter into the prepared cake pan. If using, dollop spoonfuls of the black sesame filling on top, then cover with the remaining batter.
    - Smooth the top and bake for 30-35 minutes, or until a toothpick inserted into the center comes out clean.
    - Allow the cake to cool in the pan for 10 minutes before transferring it to a wire rack to cool completely.
6. **Prepare the Frosting:**
    - In a large bowl, beat the butter until creamy. Gradually add the powdered sugar and black sesame powder, beating until smooth and fluffy.
    - Add heavy cream or milk one tablespoon at a time until the frosting reaches your desired consistency. Mix in the vanilla extract.
7. **Frost the Cake:**
    - Once the cake is completely cool, spread the black sesame frosting evenly over the cake.
    - Garnish with toasted black sesame seeds, fresh fruit, or edible flowers if desired.
8. **Serve:**
    - Slice and enjoy your homemade Black Sesame Cake!

This cake pairs wonderfully with a cup of tea and offers a rich, nutty flavor that's both unique and satisfying.

Chestnut Cake

Ingredients:

For the Cake:

- 1 cup chestnut puree (store-bought or homemade)
- 1 1/2 cups all-purpose flour
- 1 cup granulated sugar
- 1/2 cup unsalted butter, room temperature
- 2 large eggs
- 1/2 cup milk
- 1/2 cup plain yogurt (or sour cream)
- 1 1/2 tsp baking powder
- 1/2 tsp baking soda
- 1/4 tsp salt
- 1 tsp vanilla extract

For the Chestnut Frosting (optional):

- 1/2 cup chestnut puree
- 1 cup unsalted butter, room temperature
- 2 cups powdered sugar
- 2-3 tbsp heavy cream or milk
- 1 tsp vanilla extract

Optional Garnish:

- Crushed chestnuts
- Fresh fruit or edible flowers

Instructions:

1. **Prepare Chestnut Puree:**
   - If using fresh chestnuts, roast and peel them, then blend them into a smooth puree. If using canned chestnut puree, ensure it's smooth and well-mixed.
2. **Preheat Oven:**
   - Preheat your oven to 350°F (175°C). Grease and flour an 8-inch round cake pan or line it with parchment paper.
3. **Make the Cake Batter:**
   - In a medium bowl, whisk together the flour, baking powder, baking soda, and salt.
   - In a large bowl, cream the butter and granulated sugar until light and fluffy.
   - Add the eggs one at a time, beating well after each addition. Mix in the vanilla extract.
   - Add the chestnut puree and mix until well combined.

- Gradually add the dry ingredients to the butter mixture, alternating with the milk and yogurt, beginning and ending with the dry ingredients. Mix until just combined.
4. **Bake the Cake:**
    - Pour the batter into the prepared cake pan and smooth the top.
    - Bake for 30-35 minutes, or until a toothpick inserted into the center comes out clean.
    - Allow the cake to cool in the pan for 10 minutes before transferring it to a wire rack to cool completely.
5. **Prepare the Chestnut Frosting (Optional):**
    - In a large bowl, beat the butter until creamy. Gradually add the powdered sugar, mixing until smooth and fluffy.
    - Mix in the chestnut puree and vanilla extract.
    - Add heavy cream or milk one tablespoon at a time until the frosting reaches your desired consistency.
6. **Frost the Cake:**
    - Once the cake is completely cool, spread the chestnut frosting evenly over the cake.
    - Garnish with crushed chestnuts or fresh fruit if desired.
7. **Serve:**
    - Slice and enjoy your homemade Chestnut Cake!

This cake is perfect for fall or winter gatherings and pairs beautifully with a cup of coffee or tea. The chestnut flavor adds a lovely, nutty richness that makes it a special treat.

Yogurt Cake

Ingredients:

For the Cake:

- 1 cup plain yogurt (Greek or regular)
- 1 cup granulated sugar
- 1/2 cup vegetable oil or melted butter
- 2 large eggs
- 1 1/2 cups all-purpose flour
- 1 1/2 tsp baking powder
- 1/2 tsp baking soda
- 1/4 tsp salt
- 1 tsp vanilla extract
- Zest of 1 lemon (optional, for added flavor)

For the Glaze (optional):

- 1/2 cup powdered sugar
- 1-2 tbsp lemon juice or milk (adjust to desired consistency)

Optional Garnish:

- Fresh berries
- Lemon zest
- Mint leaves

Instructions:

1. **Preheat Oven:**
    - Preheat your oven to 350°F (175°C). Grease and flour an 8-inch round cake pan or line it with parchment paper.
2. **Prepare the Batter:**
    - In a large bowl, whisk together the yogurt, sugar, and vegetable oil or melted butter until smooth.
    - Add the eggs one at a time, beating well after each addition. Mix in the vanilla extract and lemon zest if using.
    - In a separate bowl, whisk together the flour, baking powder, baking soda, and salt.
    - Gradually add the dry ingredients to the wet ingredients, mixing until just combined.
3. **Bake the Cake:**
    - Pour the batter into the prepared cake pan and smooth the top.
    - Bake for 25-30 minutes, or until a toothpick inserted into the center comes out clean.

- Allow the cake to cool in the pan for 10 minutes before transferring it to a wire rack to cool completely.
4. **Prepare the Glaze (Optional):**
    - In a small bowl, whisk together the powdered sugar and lemon juice or milk until smooth. Adjust the consistency as needed by adding more liquid if necessary.
5. **Glaze and Garnish:**
    - Once the cake is completely cool, drizzle the glaze over the cake.
    - Garnish with fresh berries, additional lemon zest, or mint leaves if desired.
6. **Serve:**
    - Slice and enjoy your homemade Yogurt Cake!

This cake is versatile and can be enjoyed plain or with a variety of toppings. It's perfect for a light dessert or a sweet treat with your afternoon tea.

Honey Cake

Ingredients:

For the Cake:

- 1 cup granulated sugar
- 1/2 cup honey
- 1/2 cup unsalted butter, room temperature
- 2 large eggs
- 1 1/2 cups all-purpose flour
- 1 1/2 tsp baking powder
- 1/2 tsp baking soda
- 1/4 tsp salt
- 1/2 tsp ground cinnamon
- 1/4 tsp ground cloves
- 1/4 tsp ground nutmeg
- 1/2 cup milk
- 1 tsp vanilla extract

For the Glaze (optional):

- 1/4 cup honey
- 1/4 cup water

Optional Garnish:

- Chopped nuts (e.g., walnuts or almonds)
- Fresh fruit or edible flowers

Instructions:

1. **Preheat Oven:**
   - Preheat your oven to 350°F (175°C). Grease and flour an 8-inch round cake pan or line it with parchment paper.
2. **Prepare the Cake Batter:**
   - In a large bowl, cream together the sugar and butter until light and fluffy.
   - Add the honey and mix well.
   - Beat in the eggs one at a time, making sure each egg is fully incorporated before adding the next.
   - In a separate bowl, whisk together the flour, baking powder, baking soda, salt, cinnamon, cloves, and nutmeg.
   - Gradually add the dry ingredients to the butter mixture, alternating with the milk. Begin and end with the dry ingredients, mixing until just combined.
   - Mix in the vanilla extract.
3. **Bake the Cake:**

- Pour the batter into the prepared cake pan and smooth the top.
- Bake for 30-35 minutes, or until a toothpick inserted into the center comes out clean.
- Allow the cake to cool in the pan for 10 minutes before transferring it to a wire rack to cool completely.
4. **Prepare the Glaze (Optional):**
    - In a small saucepan, combine the honey and water. Heat over low heat until the honey is fully dissolved and the mixture is smooth.
    - Brush the glaze over the cooled cake for a shiny, sweet finish.
5. **Garnish and Serve:**
    - If desired, sprinkle the top of the cake with chopped nuts or garnish with fresh fruit or edible flowers.
    - Slice and enjoy your homemade Honey Cake!

This cake is perfect for any occasion and has a lovely, natural sweetness from the honey. It pairs wonderfully with tea or coffee and can also be enjoyed as a sweet treat on its own.

Citron Cake

Ingredients:

For the Cake:

- 1 1/2 cups all-purpose flour
- 1 cup granulated sugar
- 1/2 cup unsalted butter, room temperature
- 2 large eggs
- 1/2 cup milk
- 1/2 cup plain yogurt (or sour cream)
- 1/4 cup fresh lemon juice (or citron juice, if available)
- 2 tbsp lemon zest (or citron zest)
- 1 1/2 tsp baking powder
- 1/2 tsp baking soda
- 1/4 tsp salt
- 1 tsp vanilla extract

For the Citron Glaze:

- 1/2 cup powdered sugar
- 2-3 tbsp fresh lemon juice (or citron juice)

Optional Garnish:

- Lemon or citron zest
- Fresh fruit
- Edible flowers

Instructions:

1. **Preheat Oven:**
    - Preheat your oven to 350°F (175°C). Grease and flour an 8-inch round cake pan or line it with parchment paper.
2. **Prepare the Cake Batter:**
    - In a medium bowl, whisk together the flour, baking powder, baking soda, and salt.
    - In a large bowl, cream the butter and granulated sugar until light and fluffy.
    - Add the eggs one at a time, beating well after each addition. Mix in the vanilla extract.
    - Mix in the lemon zest and lemon juice.
    - Alternately add the dry ingredients and the milk and yogurt to the butter mixture, beginning and ending with the dry ingredients. Mix until just combined.
3. **Bake the Cake:**
    - Pour the batter into the prepared cake pan and smooth the top.

- Bake for 25-30 minutes, or until a toothpick inserted into the center comes out clean.
- Allow the cake to cool in the pan for 10 minutes before transferring it to a wire rack to cool completely.

4. **Prepare the Citron Glaze:**
    - In a small bowl, whisk together the powdered sugar and lemon juice until smooth. Adjust the consistency by adding more lemon juice if needed.
5. **Glaze and Garnish:**
    - Once the cake is completely cool, drizzle the glaze over the top of the cake.
    - Garnish with additional lemon or citron zest, fresh fruit, or edible flowers if desired.
6. **Serve:**
    - Slice and enjoy your homemade Citron Cake!

This cake is perfect for any occasion where you want a light, citrusy dessert. It's refreshing and pairs beautifully with tea or coffee.

Peach Cake

Ingredients:

For the Cake:

- 1 1/2 cups all-purpose flour
- 1 cup granulated sugar
- 1/2 cup unsalted butter, room temperature
- 2 large eggs
- 1/2 cup milk
- 1/2 cup plain yogurt (or sour cream)
- 1 tsp vanilla extract
- 1 1/2 tsp baking powder
- 1/2 tsp baking soda
- 1/4 tsp salt
- 2 cups fresh peaches, peeled, pitted, and chopped (about 3-4 medium peaches)
- 1 tbsp all-purpose flour (for coating the peaches)

For the Peach Glaze (optional):

- 1/4 cup peach preserves or jam
- 1-2 tbsp water

Optional Garnish:

- Fresh peach slices
- Powdered sugar
- Whipped cream

Instructions:

1. **Preheat Oven:**
   - Preheat your oven to 350°F (175°C). Grease and flour an 8-inch round cake pan or line it with parchment paper.
2. **Prepare the Peaches:**
   - Toss the chopped peaches with 1 tablespoon of flour. This helps to prevent the peaches from sinking to the bottom of the cake.
3. **Prepare the Cake Batter:**
   - In a medium bowl, whisk together the flour, baking powder, baking soda, and salt.
   - In a large bowl, cream the butter and granulated sugar until light and fluffy.
   - Add the eggs one at a time, beating well after each addition. Mix in the vanilla extract.
   - Alternately add the dry ingredients and the milk and yogurt to the butter mixture, beginning and ending with the dry ingredients. Mix until just combined.
   - Gently fold in the coated peaches.

4. **Bake the Cake:**
    - Pour the batter into the prepared cake pan and smooth the top.
    - Bake for 35-40 minutes, or until a toothpick inserted into the center comes out clean.
    - Allow the cake to cool in the pan for 10 minutes before transferring it to a wire rack to cool completely.
5. **Prepare the Peach Glaze (Optional):**
    - In a small saucepan, heat the peach preserves and water over low heat until smooth and slightly runny. Adjust the consistency with more water if needed.
6. **Glaze and Garnish:**
    - Once the cake is completely cool, brush the glaze over the top of the cake for a shiny finish.
    - Garnish with fresh peach slices, a dusting of powdered sugar, or a dollop of whipped cream if desired.
7. **Serve:**
    - Slice and enjoy your homemade Peach Cake!

This cake is a wonderful way to showcase fresh peaches and is perfect for summer gatherings or as a sweet treat any time of year.

Rice Cake (tteok)

Ingredients:

- 2 cups sweet rice flour (also known as glutinous rice flour or **"tteokkoji"**)
- 1 cup water
- 1/4 cup granulated sugar
- 1/4 tsp salt
- 1 tbsp vegetable oil (for greasing)

For Optional Filling:

- Red bean paste or sweetened sesame paste (if desired)

For Garnish (optional):

- Toasted sesame seeds
- Fresh fruit or edible flowers

Instructions:

1. **Prepare the Steamer:**
    - Fill a large pot or steamer with water and bring it to a boil. If using a traditional bamboo steamer, line the steamer basket with parchment paper or cheesecloth to prevent sticking.
2. **Mix the Batter:**
    - In a large bowl, combine the sweet rice flour, granulated sugar, and salt.
    - Gradually add the water, mixing continuously until you have a smooth, lump-free batter.
3. **Steam the Cake:**
    - Lightly grease a round cake pan or heatproof dish with vegetable oil.
    - Pour the batter into the prepared pan and smooth the top with a spatula.
    - Place the pan into the steamer and cover. Steam over high heat for about 20-30 minutes, or until the cake is firm and a toothpick inserted into the center comes out clean.
4. **Optional Filling:**
    - If adding a filling, such as red bean paste, you can layer some of the batter in the pan, spread a thin layer of filling on top, and then cover with the remaining batter. Steam as directed.
5. **Cool and Serve:**
    - Let the rice cake cool for a few minutes before removing it from the pan.
    - Optionally, sprinkle with toasted sesame seeds or garnish with fresh fruit or edible flowers.
6. **Slice and Enjoy:**
    - Cut into slices or small pieces and enjoy your homemade Baekseolgi Tteok!

Tips:

- Tteok can be enjoyed warm or at room temperature.
- Store leftovers in an airtight container at room temperature for up to a few days or refrigerate for longer storage. Reheat lightly before serving to restore its soft texture.

Tteok is often served during special occasions and celebrations in Korea. This basic recipe can be adapted with different fillings or toppings to suit your taste.

Kimchi Cake

Ingredients:

For the Cake:

- 1 1/2 cups all-purpose flour
- 1/2 cup cornstarch
- 1/2 cup granulated sugar
- 1 tsp baking powder
- 1/2 tsp baking soda
- 1/2 tsp salt
- 1 cup chopped kimchi (drained, with some of the juice reserved)
- 1/2 cup kimchi juice (if needed, use water if there's not enough juice)
- 1/2 cup diced onion
- 2 large eggs
- 1/2 cup vegetable oil
- 1/2 cup shredded cheese (optional, such as cheddar or mozzarella)
- 1 tbsp sesame seeds (optional)
- 2-3 green onions, chopped (for garnish)

For the Sauce (Optional):

- 2 tbsp soy sauce
- 1 tbsp rice vinegar
- 1 tbsp honey or sugar
- 1 tsp sesame oil
- 1 garlic clove, minced

Instructions:

1. **Preheat Oven:**
    - Preheat your oven to 350°F (175°C). Grease and flour an 8-inch round cake pan or line it with parchment paper.
2. **Prepare the Batter:**
    - In a large bowl, whisk together the flour, cornstarch, sugar, baking powder, baking soda, and salt.
    - In another bowl, beat the eggs and then mix in the vegetable oil.
    - Add the chopped kimchi, kimchi juice (or water), and diced onion to the wet ingredients.
    - Gradually add the wet ingredients to the dry ingredients, mixing until just combined.
    - Fold in the shredded cheese if using.
3. **Bake the Cake:**
    - Pour the batter into the prepared cake pan and smooth the top.

- Sprinkle sesame seeds on top if desired.
- Bake for 25-30 minutes, or until a toothpick inserted into the center comes out clean.
- Let the cake cool in the pan for 10 minutes before transferring it to a wire rack to cool completely.

4. **Prepare the Sauce (Optional):**
   - In a small bowl, whisk together the soy sauce, rice vinegar, honey or sugar, sesame oil, and minced garlic until well combined.
   - Serve the sauce on the side for dipping or drizzle it over the cake slices.

5. **Garnish and Serve:**
   - Garnish the cooled Kimchi Cake with chopped green onions.
   - Slice and serve as a savory snack or appetizer.

This Kimchi Cake offers a unique fusion of flavors and textures, combining the fermented tanginess of kimchi with the comforting texture of a cake. It's great for those who enjoy adventurous flavors and want to try something different with their kimchi.

\

Green Tea and Red Bean Cake

Ingredients:

For the Cake:

- 1 cup all-purpose flour
- 1 cup granulated sugar
- 1/2 cup unsalted butter, room temperature
- 2 large eggs
- 1/2 cup milk
- 1/2 cup plain yogurt (or sour cream)
- 2 tbsp matcha green tea powder
- 1 1/2 tsp baking powder
- 1/2 tsp baking soda
- 1/4 tsp salt
- 1/2 cup red bean paste (sweetened, store-bought or homemade)

For the Red Bean Swirl:

- 1/2 cup red bean paste
- 1 tbsp granulated sugar (optional, if more sweetness is desired)

For the Glaze (optional):

- 1/2 cup powdered sugar
- 2-3 tbsp milk

Optional Garnish:

- Sifted matcha powder
- Fresh berries
- Edible flowers

Instructions:

1. **Preheat Oven:**
    - Preheat your oven to 350°F (175°C). Grease and flour an 8-inch round cake pan or line it with parchment paper.
2. **Prepare the Red Bean Swirl:**
    - In a small bowl, mix 1/2 cup red bean paste with 1 tablespoon of granulated sugar if needed. Set aside.
3. **Prepare the Cake Batter:**
    - In a medium bowl, whisk together the flour, matcha green tea powder, baking powder, baking soda, and salt.
    - In a large bowl, cream the butter and granulated sugar until light and fluffy.

- Add the eggs one at a time, beating well after each addition. Mix in the vanilla extract if using.
- Add the milk and yogurt, mixing until well combined.
- Gradually add the dry ingredients to the wet ingredients, mixing until just combined.

4. **Assemble the Cake:**
    - Pour half of the batter into the prepared cake pan and smooth the top.
    - Drop spoonfuls of the red bean paste over the batter.
    - Add the remaining batter on top and smooth it out. Use a knife or skewer to swirl the red bean paste into the batter to create a marbled effect.
5. **Bake the Cake:**
    - Bake for 30-35 minutes, or until a toothpick inserted into the center comes out clean.
    - Allow the cake to cool in the pan for 10 minutes before transferring it to a wire rack to cool completely.
6. **Prepare the Glaze (Optional):**
    - In a small bowl, whisk together the powdered sugar and milk until smooth. Adjust the consistency by adding more milk if needed.
7. **Glaze and Garnish:**
    - Once the cake is completely cool, drizzle the glaze over the top.
    - Optionally, sift matcha powder over the glaze or garnish with fresh berries and edible flowers.
8. **Serve:**
    - Slice and enjoy your Green Tea and Red Bean Cake!

This cake beautifully balances the subtle bitterness of green tea with the sweet, smooth taste of red bean paste. It's perfect for those who enjoy traditional Asian flavors in a modern dessert.

Pumpkin Cake

Ingredients:

For the Cake:

- 1 1/2 cups all-purpose flour
- 1 1/2 tsp baking powder
- 1/2 tsp baking soda
- 1/2 tsp salt
- 1 tsp ground cinnamon
- 1/2 tsp ground nutmeg
- 1/4 tsp ground cloves
- 1/2 cup unsalted butter, room temperature
- 1 cup granulated sugar
- 1/2 cup packed brown sugar
- 2 large eggs
- 1 cup canned pumpkin puree (not pumpkin pie filling)
- 1/2 cup buttermilk (or milk with 1 tbsp lemon juice)
- 1 tsp vanilla extract

For the Cream Cheese Frosting:

- 1/2 cup unsalted butter, room temperature
- 8 oz cream cheese, room temperature
- 2 cups powdered sugar
- 1 tsp vanilla extract

Optional Garnish:

- Ground cinnamon
- Chopped pecans or walnuts

Instructions:

1. **Preheat Oven:**
   - Preheat your oven to 350°F (175°C). Grease and flour an 8-inch round cake pan or line it with parchment paper.
2. **Prepare the Cake Batter:**
   - In a medium bowl, whisk together the flour, baking powder, baking soda, salt, cinnamon, nutmeg, and cloves.
   - In a large bowl, cream together the butter, granulated sugar, and brown sugar until light and fluffy.
   - Add the eggs one at a time, beating well after each addition. Mix in the vanilla extract.
   - Stir in the pumpkin puree until well combined.

- Gradually add the dry ingredients to the wet ingredients, alternating with the buttermilk. Begin and end with the dry ingredients, mixing until just combined.
3. **Bake the Cake:**
    - Pour the batter into the prepared cake pan and smooth the top.
    - Bake for 30-35 minutes, or until a toothpick inserted into the center comes out clean.
    - Allow the cake to cool in the pan for 10 minutes before transferring it to a wire rack to cool completely.
4. **Prepare the Cream Cheese Frosting:**
    - In a large bowl, beat the butter and cream cheese together until creamy and smooth.
    - Gradually add the powdered sugar, beating until well combined and fluffy.
    - Mix in the vanilla extract.
5. **Frost the Cake:**
    - Once the cake is completely cool, spread the cream cheese frosting evenly over the top and sides of the cake.
    - Garnish with a sprinkle of ground cinnamon and chopped pecans or walnuts if desired.
6. **Serve:**
    - Slice and enjoy your homemade Pumpkin Cake!

This Pumpkin Cake is perfect for autumn celebrations, Thanksgiving, or anytime you want a sweet and spiced treat. The cream cheese frosting adds a rich, tangy contrast to the moist pumpkin cake.

Strawberry Cream Cake

Ingredients:

For the Cake:

- 1 1/2 cups all-purpose flour
- 1 cup granulated sugar
- 1/2 cup unsalted butter, room temperature
- 2 large eggs
- 1/2 cup milk
- 1/2 cup plain yogurt (or sour cream)
- 1 1/2 tsp baking powder
- 1/2 tsp baking soda
- 1/4 tsp salt
- 1 tsp vanilla extract
- 1 cup fresh strawberries, finely chopped

For the Strawberry Filling:

- 1 cup fresh strawberries, hulled and sliced
- 1/4 cup granulated sugar
- 1 tbsp lemon juice
- 1 tbsp cornstarch

For the Cream Frosting:

- 1 cup heavy cream
- 1/4 cup powdered sugar
- 1 tsp vanilla extract

Optional Garnish:

- Fresh strawberries
- Mint leaves
- Shaved chocolate

Instructions:

1. **Prepare the Cake:**
    - Preheat your oven to 350°F (175°C). Grease and flour an 8-inch round cake pan or line it with parchment paper.
    - In a medium bowl, whisk together the flour, baking powder, baking soda, and salt.
    - In a large bowl, cream together the butter and granulated sugar until light and fluffy.

- Add the eggs one at a time, beating well after each addition. Mix in the vanilla extract.
- Gradually add the dry ingredients to the butter mixture, alternating with the milk and yogurt. Begin and end with the dry ingredients, mixing until just combined.
- Gently fold in the finely chopped strawberries.
- Pour the batter into the prepared cake pan and smooth the top.
- Bake for 25-30 minutes, or until a toothpick inserted into the center comes out clean.
- Allow the cake to cool in the pan for 10 minutes before transferring it to a wire rack to cool completely.

2. **Prepare the Strawberry Filling:**
   - In a medium saucepan, combine the sliced strawberries, granulated sugar, lemon juice, and cornstarch.
   - Cook over medium heat, stirring frequently, until the mixture thickens and the strawberries are softened (about 5-7 minutes).
   - Allow the filling to cool completely before using.

3. **Prepare the Cream Frosting:**
   - In a large bowl, beat the heavy cream, powdered sugar, and vanilla extract until stiff peaks form.

4. **Assemble the Cake:**
   - Once the cake is completely cool, slice it in half horizontally to create two layers.
   - Spread the strawberry filling evenly over the bottom layer of the cake.
   - Place the top layer of the cake over the filling.
   - Spread the cream frosting evenly over the top and sides of the cake.

5. **Garnish and Serve:**
   - Garnish with fresh strawberries, mint leaves, or shaved chocolate if desired.
   - Slice and serve the Strawberry Cream Cake!

This Strawberry Cream Cake combines the lightness of the cake with the sweetness of fresh strawberries and the richness of cream frosting, making it a perfect dessert for any occasion. Enjoy!

Mango Cake

Ingredients:

For the Cake:

- 1 1/2 cups all-purpose flour
- 1 cup granulated sugar
- 1/2 cup unsalted butter, room temperature
- 2 large eggs
- 1/2 cup milk
- 1/2 cup mango puree (fresh or canned)
- 1 1/2 tsp baking powder
- 1/2 tsp baking soda
- 1/4 tsp salt
- 1 tsp vanilla extract

For the Mango Glaze:

- 1/2 cup mango puree
- 1/4 cup granulated sugar
- 1 tbsp cornstarch

For the Whipped Cream Frosting (optional):

- 1 cup heavy cream
- 1/4 cup powdered sugar
- 1 tsp vanilla extract

Optional Garnish:

- Fresh mango slices
- Mint leaves
- Shredded coconut

Instructions:

1. **Preheat Oven:**
    - Preheat your oven to 350°F (175°C). Grease and flour an 8-inch round cake pan or line it with parchment paper.
2. **Prepare the Cake Batter:**
    - In a medium bowl, whisk together the flour, baking powder, baking soda, and salt.
    - In a large bowl, cream together the butter and granulated sugar until light and fluffy.
    - Add the eggs one at a time, beating well after each addition. Mix in the vanilla extract.

- Gradually add the dry ingredients to the butter mixture, alternating with the milk and mango puree. Begin and end with the dry ingredients, mixing until just combined.
- Pour the batter into the prepared cake pan and smooth the top.

3. **Bake the Cake:**
   - Bake for 25-30 minutes, or until a toothpick inserted into the center comes out clean.
   - Allow the cake to cool in the pan for 10 minutes before transferring it to a wire rack to cool completely.
4. **Prepare the Mango Glaze:**
   - In a small saucepan, combine the mango puree, granulated sugar, and cornstarch.
   - Cook over medium heat, stirring frequently, until the mixture thickens and becomes glossy (about 5-7 minutes).
   - Allow the glaze to cool before using.
5. **Prepare the Whipped Cream Frosting (Optional):**
   - In a large bowl, beat the heavy cream, powdered sugar, and vanilla extract until stiff peaks form.
6. **Assemble and Frost the Cake:**
   - If desired, slice the cooled cake in half horizontally to create two layers.
   - Spread a layer of whipped cream frosting or mango glaze between the cake layers.
   - Frost the top and sides of the cake with the whipped cream frosting, or simply drizzle the mango glaze over the top.
   - Garnish with fresh mango slices, mint leaves, and shredded coconut if desired.
7. **Serve:**
   - Slice and enjoy your homemade Mango Cake!

This Mango Cake offers a light and refreshing dessert experience with the tropical flavor of mango shining through. It's perfect for summer celebrations, special occasions, or just as a delightful treat.

Choco-Chip Cake

Ingredients:

For the Cake:

- 1 1/2 cups all-purpose flour
- 1 cup granulated sugar
- 1/2 cup unsalted butter, room temperature
- 2 large eggs
- 1/2 cup milk
- 1/2 cup plain yogurt (or sour cream)
- 1 1/2 tsp baking powder
- 1/2 tsp baking soda
- 1/4 tsp salt
- 1 tsp vanilla extract
- 1 cup semi-sweet chocolate chips

For the Optional Chocolate Glaze:

- 1/2 cup semi-sweet chocolate chips
- 2 tbsp heavy cream

Optional Garnish:

- Additional chocolate chips
- Whipped cream

Instructions:

1. **Preheat Oven:**
   - Preheat your oven to 350°F (175°C). Grease and flour an 8-inch round cake pan or line it with parchment paper.
2. **Prepare the Cake Batter:**
   - In a medium bowl, whisk together the flour, baking powder, baking soda, and salt.
   - In a large bowl, cream together the butter and granulated sugar until light and fluffy.
   - Add the eggs one at a time, beating well after each addition. Mix in the vanilla extract.
   - Gradually add the dry ingredients to the butter mixture, alternating with the milk and yogurt. Begin and end with the dry ingredients, mixing until just combined.
   - Fold in the chocolate chips gently.
3. **Bake the Cake:**
   - Pour the batter into the prepared cake pan and smooth the top.
   - Bake for 25-30 minutes, or until a toothpick inserted into the center comes out clean.

- Allow the cake to cool in the pan for 10 minutes before transferring it to a wire rack to cool completely.
4. **Prepare the Chocolate Glaze (Optional):**
   - In a small saucepan, heat the heavy cream over low heat until just starting to simmer.
   - Remove from heat and add the chocolate chips. Stir until smooth and melted.
   - Let the glaze cool slightly before drizzling over the cake.
5. **Frost and Garnish:**
   - If using the chocolate glaze, drizzle it over the cooled cake and let it set.
   - Garnish with additional chocolate chips or whipped cream if desired.
6. **Serve:**
   - Slice and enjoy your homemade Choco-Chip Cake!

This Choco-Chip Cake is a comforting dessert with a rich chocolate flavor and a soft, moist texture. It's perfect for chocolate lovers and is sure to be a hit at any gathering.

Jujube Cake

Ingredients:

For the Cake:

- 1 1/2 cups all-purpose flour
- 1 cup granulated sugar
- 1/2 cup unsalted butter, room temperature
- 2 large eggs
- 1/2 cup milk
- 1/2 cup jujube paste or chopped dried jujubes (see note below)
- 1 1/2 tsp baking powder
- 1/2 tsp baking soda
- 1/4 tsp salt
- 1 tsp vanilla extract
- 1/2 tsp ground cinnamon (optional, for extra flavor)

For the Glaze (optional):

- 1/4 cup jujube syrup or honey
- 1 tbsp water

Optional Garnish:

- Sliced jujubes
- Powdered sugar

Instructions:

1. **Prepare the Jujube Paste (if using dried jujubes):**
   - If using dried jujubes, chop them into small pieces and soak them in warm water for about 30 minutes to soften. Drain and chop finely or blend into a paste.
2. **Preheat Oven:**
   - Preheat your oven to 350°F (175°C). Grease and flour an 8-inch round cake pan or line it with parchment paper.
3. **Prepare the Cake Batter:**
   - In a medium bowl, whisk together the flour, baking powder, baking soda, salt, and ground cinnamon if using.
   - In a large bowl, cream together the butter and granulated sugar until light and fluffy.
   - Add the eggs one at a time, beating well after each addition. Mix in the vanilla extract.
   - Gradually add the dry ingredients to the butter mixture, alternating with the milk. Begin and end with the dry ingredients, mixing until just combined.
   - Fold in the jujube paste or chopped jujubes.

4. **Bake the Cake:**
   - Pour the batter into the prepared cake pan and smooth the top.
   - Bake for 25-30 minutes, or until a toothpick inserted into the center comes out clean.
   - Allow the cake to cool in the pan for 10 minutes before transferring it to a wire rack to cool completely.
5. **Prepare the Glaze (Optional):**
   - In a small saucepan, heat the jujube syrup or honey with 1 tablespoon of water over low heat until slightly warmed and thinned. Brush or drizzle over the cooled cake.
6. **Garnish and Serve:**
   - Garnish with sliced jujubes and a dusting of powdered sugar if desired.
7. **Enjoy:**
   - Slice and enjoy your Jujube Cake!

Notes:

- **Jujube Paste:** You can find jujube paste at Asian grocery stores, or you can make it by blending softened jujubes into a smooth paste.
- **Jujube Syrup:** Jujube syrup can also be found at Asian markets or online. If unavailable, honey can be used as an alternative.

Jujube Cake has a unique flavor profile that combines the natural sweetness and depth of jujubes with a soft, moist cake. It's a wonderful way to enjoy this distinctive fruit in a baked treat.

Cinnamon Cake

Ingredients:

For the Cake:

- 1 1/2 cups all-purpose flour
- 1 cup granulated sugar
- 1/2 cup unsalted butter, room temperature
- 2 large eggs
- 1/2 cup milk
- 1/2 cup plain yogurt (or sour cream)
- 1 1/2 tsp baking powder
- 1/2 tsp baking soda
- 1/4 tsp salt
- 2 tsp ground cinnamon
- 1 tsp vanilla extract

For the Cinnamon Swirl:

- 1/4 cup granulated sugar
- 1 tbsp ground cinnamon
- 1 tbsp unsalted butter, melted

For the Glaze (optional):

- 1/2 cup powdered sugar
- 2-3 tbsp milk
- 1/2 tsp vanilla extract

Optional Garnish:

- Additional ground cinnamon
- Chopped nuts

Instructions:

1. **Preheat Oven:**
   - Preheat your oven to 350°F (175°C). Grease and flour an 8-inch round cake pan or line it with parchment paper.
2. **Prepare the Cinnamon Swirl:**
   - In a small bowl, mix together the granulated sugar, ground cinnamon, and melted butter. Set aside.
3. **Prepare the Cake Batter:**
   - In a medium bowl, whisk together the flour, baking powder, baking soda, salt, and ground cinnamon.

- In a large bowl, cream together the butter and granulated sugar until light and fluffy.
- Add the eggs one at a time, beating well after each addition. Mix in the vanilla extract.
- Gradually add the dry ingredients to the butter mixture, alternating with the milk and yogurt. Begin and end with the dry ingredients, mixing until just combined.

4. **Assemble the Cake:**
    - Pour half of the cake batter into the prepared cake pan and smooth the top.
    - Sprinkle half of the cinnamon swirl mixture evenly over the batter.
    - Add the remaining cake batter on top and smooth the surface.
    - Sprinkle the remaining cinnamon swirl mixture over the top of the cake.
    - Use a knife or skewer to gently swirl the cinnamon mixture into the batter to create a marble effect.
5. **Bake the Cake:**
    - Bake for 30-35 minutes, or until a toothpick inserted into the center comes out clean.
    - Allow the cake to cool in the pan for 10 minutes before transferring it to a wire rack to cool completely.
6. **Prepare the Glaze (Optional):**
    - In a small bowl, whisk together the powdered sugar, milk, and vanilla extract until smooth. Adjust the consistency with more milk or powdered sugar if needed.
7. **Glaze and Garnish:**
    - Once the cake is completely cool, drizzle the glaze over the top.
    - Optionally, sprinkle with additional ground cinnamon or chopped nuts.
8. **Serve:**
    - Slice and enjoy your homemade Cinnamon Cake!

This Cinnamon Cake is wonderfully aromatic with a perfect balance of sweetness and spice. It's great as a dessert or a treat with your afternoon coffee or tea.

Almond Cake

Ingredients:

For the Cake:

- 1 cup all-purpose flour
- 1 cup almond flour (or finely ground almonds)
- 1 cup granulated sugar
- 1/2 cup unsalted butter, room temperature
- 3 large eggs
- 1/2 cup milk
- 1/2 tsp baking powder
- 1/4 tsp salt
- 1 tsp almond extract
- 1/2 tsp vanilla extract

For the Almond Glaze (Optional):

- 1/2 cup powdered sugar
- 2-3 tbsp milk
- 1/2 tsp almond extract

Optional Garnish:

- Sliced almonds
- Powdered sugar

Instructions:

1. **Preheat Oven:**
   - Preheat your oven to 350°F (175°C). Grease and flour an 8-inch round cake pan or line it with parchment paper.
2. **Prepare the Cake Batter:**
   - In a medium bowl, whisk together the all-purpose flour, almond flour, baking powder, and salt.
   - In a large bowl, cream together the butter and granulated sugar until light and fluffy.
   - Add the eggs one at a time, beating well after each addition. Mix in the almond extract and vanilla extract.
   - Gradually add the dry ingredients to the butter mixture, alternating with the milk. Begin and end with the dry ingredients, mixing until just combined.
3. **Bake the Cake:**
   - Pour the batter into the prepared cake pan and smooth the top.
   - Bake for 30-35 minutes, or until a toothpick inserted into the center comes out clean.

- Allow the cake to cool in the pan for 10 minutes before transferring it to a wire rack to cool completely.
4. **Prepare the Almond Glaze (Optional):**
    - In a small bowl, whisk together the powdered sugar, milk, and almond extract until smooth. Adjust the consistency with more milk or powdered sugar if needed.
5. **Glaze and Garnish:**
    - Once the cake is completely cool, drizzle the almond glaze over the top.
    - Garnish with sliced almonds and a dusting of powdered sugar if desired.
6. **Serve:**
    - Slice and enjoy your homemade Almond Cake!

Tips:

- **Almond Flour:** If you don't have almond flour, you can make your own by finely grinding blanched almonds in a food processor. Just be careful not to grind them into almond butter.
- **Flavor Variations:** You can also add a bit of lemon zest or orange zest to the batter for a citrusy twist.

This Almond Cake is moist, nutty, and subtly sweet, with the almond flavor shining through. It pairs beautifully with tea or coffee and makes a great addition to any dessert table.

Spicy Rice Cake Cake

Ingredients:

For the Rice Cake Base:

- 1 cup rice flour
- 1 cup water
- 1/4 cup granulated sugar
- 1/2 tsp salt

For the Spicy Sauce:

- 1/4 cup gochujang (Korean red chili paste)
- 2 tbsp soy sauce
- 2 tbsp honey or sugar
- 1 tbsp sesame oil
- 1 garlic clove, minced
- 1 tsp ginger, minced

For the Cake Assembly:

- 1/2 cup cooked rice cakes (tteokbokki rice cakes, either store-bought or homemade, cut into small pieces)
- 1/4 cup chopped green onions
- 1/4 cup sesame seeds (optional)

For Garnish (Optional):

- Chopped scallions
- Sesame seeds
- Fresh cilantro or parsley

Instructions:

1. **Prepare the Rice Cake Base:**
    - In a medium bowl, combine rice flour, water, granulated sugar, and salt. Mix well until smooth.
    - Pour the mixture into a greased 8-inch round cake pan. Smooth the surface.
    - Steam the mixture for about 20-25 minutes, or until set and firm. Allow to cool completely before removing from the pan.
2. **Prepare the Spicy Sauce:**
    - In a small saucepan, combine gochujang, soy sauce, honey (or sugar), sesame oil, minced garlic, and minced ginger.
    - Cook over medium heat, stirring frequently, until the sauce is well combined and slightly thickened (about 5 minutes). Allow to cool slightly.

3. **Assemble the Cake:**
   - Once the rice cake base is completely cooled, remove it from the pan and place it on a serving plate.
   - Gently fold the cooked rice cake pieces into the slightly cooled spicy sauce.
   - Spread the spicy rice cake mixture evenly over the top of the rice cake base.
   - Garnish with chopped green onions and sesame seeds if desired.
4. **Garnish and Serve:**
   - Optionally, garnish with additional chopped scallions, sesame seeds, and fresh cilantro or parsley.
   - Slice and serve. Enjoy the spicy and savory flavors of your Spicy Rice Cake Cake!

Notes:

- **Rice Cake Texture:** If the rice cake base is too chewy for your liking, you can adjust the texture by steaming for a shorter or longer time, depending on your preference.
- **Adjusting Spice Level:** Adjust the amount of gochujang to suit your spice tolerance. You can also add a little bit of red pepper flakes for extra heat.

This Spicy Rice Cake Cake is a unique twist on traditional rice cakes and offers a deliciously spicy and savory flavor profile. It's perfect for those who enjoy a fusion of sweet and spicy in a cake form!

Coconut Cake

Ingredients:

For the Cake:

- 1 1/2 cups all-purpose flour
- 1 1/2 tsp baking powder
- 1/2 tsp baking soda
- 1/4 tsp salt
- 1/2 cup unsalted butter, room temperature
- 1 cup granulated sugar
- 2 large eggs
- 1/2 cup milk
- 1/2 cup coconut milk
- 1 cup shredded coconut (sweetened or unsweetened, depending on your preference)
- 1 tsp vanilla extract
- 1/2 tsp almond extract (optional, for added flavor)

For the Coconut Frosting:

- 1/2 cup unsalted butter, room temperature
- 4 oz cream cheese, room temperature
- 2 1/2 cups powdered sugar
- 1/4 cup coconut milk (or regular milk)
- 1 tsp vanilla extract
- 1 cup shredded coconut (for garnish)

Optional Garnish:

- Toasted coconut flakes
- Fresh coconut slices
- Maraschino cherries

Instructions:

1. **Preheat Oven:**
   - Preheat your oven to 350°F (175°C). Grease and flour two 8-inch round cake pans or line them with parchment paper.
2. **Prepare the Cake Batter:**
   - In a medium bowl, whisk together the flour, baking powder, baking soda, and salt.
   - In a large bowl, cream together the butter and granulated sugar until light and fluffy.
   - Add the eggs one at a time, beating well after each addition. Mix in the vanilla extract and almond extract if using.

- Gradually add the dry ingredients to the butter mixture, alternating with the milk and coconut milk. Begin and end with the dry ingredients, mixing until just combined.
- Fold in the shredded coconut.

3. **Bake the Cake:**
   - Divide the batter evenly between the prepared cake pans and smooth the tops.
   - Bake for 25-30 minutes, or until a toothpick inserted into the center comes out clean.
   - Allow the cakes to cool in the pans for 10 minutes before transferring them to a wire rack to cool completely.

4. **Prepare the Coconut Frosting:**
   - In a large bowl, beat the butter and cream cheese together until creamy and smooth.
   - Gradually add the powdered sugar, beating until well combined.
   - Mix in the coconut milk and vanilla extract until the frosting is smooth and spreadable.

5. **Assemble and Frost the Cake:**
   - Once the cakes are completely cooled, place one cake layer on a serving plate or cake stand.
   - Spread a layer of coconut frosting on top.
   - Place the second cake layer on top and frost the top and sides of the cake with the remaining coconut frosting.
   - Garnish with shredded coconut and toasted coconut flakes if desired.

6. **Serve:**
   - Slice and enjoy your homemade Coconut Cake!

Tips:

- **Toasting Coconut:** Toasted coconut adds extra flavor and crunch. To toast shredded coconut, place it in a dry skillet over medium heat, stirring frequently, until golden brown.
- **Coconut Milk:** For a more intense coconut flavor, use full-fat coconut milk.

This Coconut Cake is a delightful dessert with a soft texture and rich coconut flavor, making it a favorite for celebrations and special occasions.

Lemon Cake

Ingredients:

For the Cake:

- 1 1/2 cups all-purpose flour
- 1 cup granulated sugar
- 1/2 cup unsalted butter, room temperature
- 2 large eggs
- 1/2 cup milk
- 1/4 cup fresh lemon juice
- 1 tablespoon lemon zest
- 1 1/2 tsp baking powder
- 1/2 tsp baking soda
- 1/4 tsp salt
- 1 tsp vanilla extract

For the Lemon Glaze (Optional):

- 1 cup powdered sugar
- 2-3 tbsp fresh lemon juice
- 1 tsp lemon zest

For the Lemon Frosting (Optional):

- 1/2 cup unsalted butter, room temperature
- 4 oz cream cheese, room temperature
- 2 1/2 cups powdered sugar
- 2-3 tbsp fresh lemon juice
- 1 tsp lemon zest

Optional Garnish:

- Lemon slices
- Lemon zest
- Fresh mint leaves

Instructions:

1. **Preheat Oven:**
    - Preheat your oven to 350°F (175°C). Grease and flour an 8-inch round cake pan or line it with parchment paper.
2. **Prepare the Cake Batter:**
    - In a medium bowl, whisk together the flour, baking powder, baking soda, and salt.

- In a large bowl, cream together the butter and granulated sugar until light and fluffy.
- Add the eggs one at a time, beating well after each addition. Mix in the vanilla extract, lemon juice, and lemon zest.
- Gradually add the dry ingredients to the butter mixture, alternating with the milk. Begin and end with the dry ingredients, mixing until just combined.

3. **Bake the Cake:**
   - Pour the batter into the prepared cake pan and smooth the top.
   - Bake for 25-30 minutes, or until a toothpick inserted into the center comes out clean.
   - Allow the cake to cool in the pan for 10 minutes before transferring it to a wire rack to cool completely.

4. **Prepare the Lemon Glaze (Optional):**
   - In a small bowl, whisk together the powdered sugar, lemon juice, and lemon zest until smooth. Adjust the consistency with more lemon juice or powdered sugar if needed.
   - Drizzle over the cooled cake.

5. **Prepare the Lemon Frosting (Optional):**
   - In a large bowl, beat the butter and cream cheese together until creamy.
   - Gradually add the powdered sugar, beating until smooth.
   - Mix in the lemon juice and lemon zest until well combined.
   - Frost the cooled cake with the lemon frosting.

6. **Garnish and Serve:**
   - Optionally, garnish with lemon slices, additional lemon zest, or fresh mint leaves.
   - Slice and enjoy your homemade Lemon Cake!

Tips:

- **Lemon Zest:** For the best flavor, use freshly grated lemon zest.
- **Lemon Juice:** Fresh lemon juice gives the best flavor, but bottled lemon juice can be used in a pinch.
- **Cake Moistness:** For extra moistness, you can brush the cooled cake with a lemon simple syrup (made by simmering equal parts sugar and water with a bit of lemon juice).

This Lemon Cake is light, tangy, and sweet, making it a perfect dessert for spring and summer or anytime you need a refreshing treat.

Maple Cake

Ingredients:

For the Cake:

- 1 1/2 cups all-purpose flour
- 1 cup granulated sugar
- 1/2 cup unsalted butter, room temperature
- 2 large eggs
- 1/2 cup pure maple syrup
- 1/2 cup milk
- 1 1/2 tsp baking powder
- 1/2 tsp baking soda
- 1/4 tsp salt
- 1 tsp vanilla extract

For the Maple Glaze (Optional):

- 1/2 cup pure maple syrup
- 1/4 cup heavy cream
- 1 tbsp unsalted butter
- 1/2 tsp vanilla extract

For the Maple Frosting (Optional):

- 1/2 cup unsalted butter, room temperature
- 2 cups powdered sugar
- 1/4 cup pure maple syrup
- 1-2 tbsp milk (if needed)
- 1/2 tsp vanilla extract

Optional Garnish:

- Chopped nuts (like walnuts or pecans)
- Additional maple syrup

Instructions:

1. **Preheat Oven:**
    - Preheat your oven to 350°F (175°C). Grease and flour an 8-inch round cake pan or line it with parchment paper.
2. **Prepare the Cake Batter:**
    - In a medium bowl, whisk together the flour, baking powder, baking soda, and salt.
    - In a large bowl, cream together the butter and granulated sugar until light and fluffy.

- Add the eggs one at a time, beating well after each addition. Mix in the vanilla extract and maple syrup.
    - Gradually add the dry ingredients to the butter mixture, alternating with the milk. Begin and end with the dry ingredients, mixing until just combined.
3. **Bake the Cake:**
    - Pour the batter into the prepared cake pan and smooth the top.
    - Bake for 25-30 minutes, or until a toothpick inserted into the center comes out clean.
    - Allow the cake to cool in the pan for 10 minutes before transferring it to a wire rack to cool completely.
4. **Prepare the Maple Glaze (Optional):**
    - In a small saucepan, combine the maple syrup, heavy cream, and butter. Heat over medium heat until the mixture is smooth and slightly thickened (about 5 minutes).
    - Remove from heat and stir in the vanilla extract.
    - Allow the glaze to cool slightly before drizzling over the cooled cake.
5. **Prepare the Maple Frosting (Optional):**
    - In a large bowl, beat the butter until creamy.
    - Gradually add the powdered sugar, beating until well combined.
    - Mix in the maple syrup and vanilla extract until smooth. Adjust the consistency with milk if needed.
    - Frost the cooled cake with the maple frosting.
6. **Garnish and Serve:**
    - Optionally, garnish with chopped nuts and a drizzle of additional maple syrup.
    - Slice and enjoy your homemade Maple Cake!

Tips:

- **Maple Syrup:** Use pure maple syrup for the best flavor. Avoid imitation maple syrup, as it can affect the taste and quality of the cake.
- **Texture:** For a moister cake, you can brush the cooled cake with a bit of maple syrup before frosting or glazing.

This Maple Cake offers a sweet, warm flavor with a lovely maple aroma, making it a comforting and delightful dessert choice.

Vanilla Cream Cake

Ingredients:

For the Cake:

- 1 1/2 cups all-purpose flour
- 1 1/2 tsp baking powder
- 1/2 tsp baking soda
- 1/4 tsp salt
- 1/2 cup unsalted butter, room temperature
- 1 cup granulated sugar
- 2 large eggs
- 1/2 cup sour cream or plain yogurt
- 1/2 cup milk
- 2 tsp vanilla extract

For the Vanilla Cream Frosting:

- 1/2 cup unsalted butter, room temperature
- 4 oz cream cheese, room temperature
- 2 1/2 cups powdered sugar
- 2 tbsp heavy cream or milk
- 1 tsp vanilla extract

Optional Garnish:

- Fresh berries (such as strawberries or raspberries)
- Edible flowers
- Sprinkles

Instructions:

1. **Preheat Oven:**
    - Preheat your oven to 350°F (175°C). Grease and flour two 8-inch round cake pans or line them with parchment paper.
2. **Prepare the Cake Batter:**
    - In a medium bowl, whisk together the flour, baking powder, baking soda, and salt.
    - In a large bowl, cream together the butter and granulated sugar until light and fluffy.
    - Add the eggs one at a time, beating well after each addition. Mix in the vanilla extract.
    - Gradually add the dry ingredients to the butter mixture, alternating with the sour cream (or yogurt) and milk. Begin and end with the dry ingredients, mixing until just combined.
3. **Bake the Cake:**

- Divide the batter evenly between the prepared cake pans and smooth the tops.
- Bake for 25-30 minutes, or until a toothpick inserted into the center comes out clean.
- Allow the cakes to cool in the pans for 10 minutes before transferring them to a wire rack to cool completely.

4. **Prepare the Vanilla Cream Frosting:**
    - In a large bowl, beat the butter and cream cheese together until creamy and smooth.
    - Gradually add the powdered sugar, beating until well combined.
    - Mix in the heavy cream (or milk) and vanilla extract until the frosting is smooth and spreadable.

5. **Assemble and Frost the Cake:**
    - Once the cakes are completely cooled, place one layer on a serving plate or cake stand.
    - Spread a layer of vanilla cream frosting on top of the first layer.
    - Place the second cake layer on top and frost the top and sides of the cake with the remaining vanilla cream frosting.

6. **Garnish and Serve:**
    - Optionally, garnish with fresh berries, edible flowers, or sprinkles.
    - Slice and enjoy your Vanilla Cream Cake!

Tips:

- **Sour Cream or Yogurt:** Using sour cream or yogurt in the cake batter helps to keep the cake moist and adds a slight tanginess that balances the sweetness.
- **Frosting Consistency:** If the frosting is too thick, you can add a little more heavy cream or milk. If it's too thin, add more powdered sugar until the desired consistency is reached.

This Vanilla Cream Cake is light, fluffy, and decadently creamy, making it a classic favorite for any cake lover.

Ginger Cake

Ingredients:

For the Cake:

- 1 1/2 cups all-purpose flour
- 1 cup granulated sugar
- 1/2 cup unsalted butter, room temperature
- 1/2 cup molasses (preferably dark or robust)
- 1/2 cup hot water
- 1 large egg
- 1 tsp ground ginger
- 1/2 tsp ground cinnamon
- 1/2 tsp ground cloves
- 1/2 tsp baking powder
- 1/2 tsp baking soda
- 1/4 tsp salt

For the Ginger Glaze (Optional):

- 1/2 cup powdered sugar
- 2-3 tbsp water or milk
- 1/2 tsp ground ginger (or fresh grated ginger for extra flavor)

For the Ginger Frosting (Optional):

- 1/2 cup unsalted butter, room temperature
- 2 cups powdered sugar
- 2 tbsp molasses
- 1-2 tbsp milk or heavy cream
- 1/2 tsp ground ginger

Optional Garnish:

- Crystallized ginger pieces
- Freshly grated ginger
- Powdered sugar

Instructions:

1. **Preheat Oven:**
   - Preheat your oven to 350°F (175°C). Grease and flour an 8-inch round or square cake pan, or line it with parchment paper.
2. **Prepare the Cake Batter:**

- In a medium bowl, whisk together the flour, ground ginger, cinnamon, cloves, baking powder, baking soda, and salt.
- In a large bowl, cream together the butter and granulated sugar until light and fluffy.
- Add the egg and mix until well combined.
- Gradually add the molasses, mixing until smooth.
- Alternately add the dry ingredients and hot water to the butter mixture, beginning and ending with the dry ingredients. Mix until just combined.

3. **Bake the Cake:**
   - Pour the batter into the prepared cake pan and smooth the top.
   - Bake for 30-35 minutes, or until a toothpick inserted into the center comes out clean.
   - Allow the cake to cool in the pan for 10 minutes before transferring it to a wire rack to cool completely.
4. **Prepare the Ginger Glaze (Optional):**
   - In a small bowl, whisk together the powdered sugar, water (or milk), and ground ginger until smooth. Adjust the consistency with more liquid or powdered sugar if needed.
   - Drizzle the glaze over the cooled cake.
5. **Prepare the Ginger Frosting (Optional):**
   - In a large bowl, beat the butter until creamy.
   - Gradually add the powdered sugar, beating until smooth.
   - Mix in the molasses, milk (or cream), and ground ginger until well combined. Adjust the consistency with more milk or powdered sugar if needed.
   - Frost the cooled cake with the ginger frosting.
6. **Garnish and Serve:**
   - Optionally, garnish with pieces of crystallized ginger, freshly grated ginger, or a dusting of powdered sugar.
   - Slice and enjoy your homemade Ginger Cake!

Tips:

- **Molasses:** Using dark molasses gives the cake a richer flavor. If you don't have molasses, you can substitute with honey or golden syrup, though it will slightly change the taste.
- **Spice Level:** Adjust the amount of ground ginger, cinnamon, and cloves to suit your taste preferences.

This Ginger Cake is wonderfully spiced and has a moist, tender crumb, making it a comforting and flavorful dessert that's sure to please!

Black Bean Cake

Ingredients:

For the Cake:

- 1 cup black beans (cooked and drained, or canned black beans, rinsed and drained)
- 1/2 cup granulated sugar
- 1/2 cup all-purpose flour
- 1/4 cup unsweetened cocoa powder
- 1/4 cup coconut oil or vegetable oil
- 2 large eggs
- 1/2 tsp vanilla extract
- 1/2 tsp baking powder
- 1/4 tsp baking soda
- 1/4 tsp salt

For the Optional Glaze or Topping:

- 1/2 cup powdered sugar
- 2-3 tbsp milk
- 1/2 tsp vanilla extract

Optional Garnish:

- Fresh berries
- Shredded coconut
- Whipped cream or yogurt

Instructions:

1. **Prepare the Black Beans:**
   - If using canned black beans, rinse and drain them well. If using cooked black beans, ensure they are well-drained.
2. **Preheat Oven:**
   - Preheat your oven to 350°F (175°C). Grease and flour an 8-inch round cake pan or line it with parchment paper.
3. **Prepare the Cake Batter:**
   - In a food processor, blend the black beans until smooth. You may need to add a little water to help with blending, but the mixture should be thick.
   - Add the sugar, cocoa powder, and oil to the blended black beans and pulse until well combined.
   - Add the eggs one at a time, blending well after each addition. Mix in the vanilla extract.
   - In a separate bowl, whisk together the flour, baking powder, baking soda, and salt.

- Gradually add the dry ingredients to the bean mixture, blending until just combined.
4. **Bake the Cake:**
   - Pour the batter into the prepared cake pan and smooth the top.
   - Bake for 25-30 minutes, or until a toothpick inserted into the center comes out clean.
   - Allow the cake to cool in the pan for 10 minutes before transferring it to a wire rack to cool completely.
5. **Prepare the Optional Glaze or Topping (if using):**
   - In a small bowl, whisk together the powdered sugar, milk, and vanilla extract until smooth. Adjust the consistency with more milk or powdered sugar if needed.
   - Drizzle over the cooled cake.
6. **Garnish and Serve:**
   - Optionally, garnish with fresh berries, shredded coconut, or a dollop of whipped cream or yogurt.
   - Slice and enjoy your homemade Sweet Black Bean Cake!

Tips:

- **Texture:** For a smoother cake, ensure the black beans are fully blended. If the batter is too thick, add a small amount of water or milk to adjust.
- **Flavor:** This cake has a subtle bean flavor complemented by cocoa and vanilla. It pairs well with fruits or light toppings.

Sweet Black Bean Cake is a nutritious and slightly different take on traditional cakes, offering a unique texture and flavor profile that can be both satisfying and surprising!

Sesame and Honey Cake

Ingredients:

For the Cake:

- 1 cup all-purpose flour
- 1/2 cup sesame seeds (toasted)
- 1/2 cup granulated sugar
- 1/4 cup honey
- 1/2 cup unsalted butter, room temperature
- 2 large eggs
- 1/2 cup milk
- 1 tsp baking powder
- 1/2 tsp baking soda
- 1/4 tsp salt
- 1/2 tsp vanilla extract

For the Honey Glaze (Optional):

- 1/4 cup honey
- 1-2 tbsp water (to thin, if necessary)
- 1/2 tsp lemon juice (optional, for a bit of tang)

Optional Garnish:

- Toasted sesame seeds
- Fresh fruit (such as berries or sliced figs)

Instructions:

1. **Preheat Oven:**
    - Preheat your oven to 350°F (175°C). Grease and flour an 8-inch round cake pan or line it with parchment paper.
2. **Prepare the Sesame Seeds:**
    - Toast the sesame seeds in a dry skillet over medium heat until they are golden and fragrant. Allow them to cool before using.
3. **Prepare the Cake Batter:**
    - In a medium bowl, whisk together the flour, baking powder, baking soda, and salt.
    - In a large bowl, cream together the butter and granulated sugar until light and fluffy.
    - Add the eggs one at a time, beating well after each addition. Mix in the vanilla extract and honey.
    - Gradually add the dry ingredients to the butter mixture, alternating with the milk. Begin and end with the dry ingredients, mixing until just combined.
    - Fold in the toasted sesame seeds.

4. **Bake the Cake:**
    - Pour the batter into the prepared cake pan and smooth the top.
    - Bake for 25-30 minutes, or until a toothpick inserted into the center comes out clean.
    - Allow the cake to cool in the pan for 10 minutes before transferring it to a wire rack to cool completely.
5. **Prepare the Honey Glaze (Optional):**
    - In a small saucepan, heat the honey over low heat until it becomes slightly runny. If needed, add water a little at a time to achieve the desired consistency.
    - Stir in the lemon juice if using.
    - Drizzle the glaze over the cooled cake.
6. **Garnish and Serve:**
    - Optionally, garnish with additional toasted sesame seeds and fresh fruit.
    - Slice and enjoy your homemade Sesame and Honey Cake!

Tips:

- **Toasting Sesame Seeds:** Toasting the sesame seeds enhances their flavor and adds a lovely crunch to the cake.
- **Honey Consistency:** If the honey is too thick, gently warm it up to make it easier to drizzle.

Sesame and Honey Cake is a unique and flavorful dessert that pairs well with a cup of tea or coffee. Its combination of sweet honey and nutty sesame seeds creates a deliciously satisfying treat!

Lychee Cake

Ingredients:

For the Cake:

- 1 1/2 cups all-purpose flour
- 1 cup granulated sugar
- 1/2 cup unsalted butter, room temperature
- 2 large eggs
- 1/2 cup canned lychee (drained, chopped)
- 1/2 cup lychee juice (from the canned lychee or store-bought)
- 1/2 cup milk
- 1 1/2 tsp baking powder
- 1/2 tsp baking soda
- 1/4 tsp salt
- 1 tsp vanilla extract

For the Lychee Frosting:

- 1/2 cup unsalted butter, room temperature
- 4 oz cream cheese, room temperature
- 2 1/2 cups powdered sugar
- 1/4 cup lychee juice
- 1/2 tsp vanilla extract

Optional Garnish:

- Fresh lychee fruit (peeled and sliced)
- Mint leaves
- Edible flowers

Instructions:

1. **Preheat Oven:**
    - Preheat your oven to 350°F (175°C). Grease and flour an 8-inch round cake pan or line it with parchment paper.
2. **Prepare the Cake Batter:**
    - In a medium bowl, whisk together the flour, baking powder, baking soda, and salt.
    - In a large bowl, cream together the butter and granulated sugar until light and fluffy.
    - Add the eggs one at a time, beating well after each addition. Mix in the vanilla extract.
    - Gradually add the dry ingredients to the butter mixture, alternating with the milk and lychee juice. Begin and end with the dry ingredients, mixing until just combined.

- Fold in the chopped lychee pieces.
3. **Bake the Cake:**
    - Pour the batter into the prepared cake pan and smooth the top.
    - Bake for 25-30 minutes, or until a toothpick inserted into the center comes out clean.
    - Allow the cake to cool in the pan for 10 minutes before transferring it to a wire rack to cool completely.
4. **Prepare the Lychee Frosting:**
    - In a large bowl, beat the butter and cream cheese together until creamy and smooth.
    - Gradually add the powdered sugar, beating until well combined.
    - Mix in the lychee juice and vanilla extract until the frosting is smooth and spreadable.
5. **Assemble and Frost the Cake:**
    - Once the cake is completely cooled, place one layer on a serving plate or cake stand.
    - Spread a layer of lychee frosting on top of the first layer.
    - Place the second cake layer on top and frost the top and sides of the cake with the remaining lychee frosting.
6. **Garnish and Serve:**
    - Optionally, garnish with fresh lychee slices, mint leaves, or edible flowers.
    - Slice and enjoy your homemade Lychee Cake!

Tips:

- **Lychee Juice:** If you can't find lychee juice, you can substitute with coconut water or fruit juice of your choice for a different but still delicious flavor.
- **Texture:** For a smoother texture, you can blend the lychee fruit into a puree before adding it to the cake batter.

Lychee Cake offers a tropical twist to traditional cakes with its sweet, floral flavor and soft, moist crumb. It's perfect for special occasions or as a refreshing treat.

Blueberry Cake

Ingredients:

For the Cake:

- 1 1/2 cups all-purpose flour
- 1 cup granulated sugar
- 1/2 cup unsalted butter, room temperature
- 2 large eggs
- 1/2 cup milk
- 1 tsp vanilla extract
- 1 1/2 tsp baking powder
- 1/2 tsp baking soda
- 1/4 tsp salt
- 1 cup fresh or frozen blueberries (if using frozen, do not thaw)

For the Blueberry Glaze (Optional):

- 1/2 cup powdered sugar
- 2-3 tbsp fresh blueberry juice (or use water if blueberry juice is not available)
- 1/2 tsp lemon juice (optional)

For the Blueberry Frosting (Optional):

- 1/2 cup unsalted butter, room temperature
- 4 oz cream cheese, room temperature
- 2 cups powdered sugar
- 1/4 cup fresh blueberry puree (blend fresh or thawed frozen blueberries)
- 1/2 tsp vanilla extract

Optional Garnish:

- Fresh blueberries
- Lemon zest
- Mint leaves

Instructions:

1. **Preheat Oven:**
    - Preheat your oven to 350°F (175°C). Grease and flour an 8-inch round cake pan or line it with parchment paper.
2. **Prepare the Cake Batter:**
    - In a medium bowl, whisk together the flour, baking powder, baking soda, and salt.
    - In a large bowl, cream together the butter and granulated sugar until light and fluffy.

- Add the eggs one at a time, beating well after each addition. Mix in the vanilla extract.
- Gradually add the dry ingredients to the butter mixture, alternating with the milk. Begin and end with the dry ingredients, mixing until just combined.
- Gently fold in the blueberries.
3. **Bake the Cake:**
    - Pour the batter into the prepared cake pan and smooth the top.
    - Bake for 25-30 minutes, or until a toothpick inserted into the center comes out clean.
    - Allow the cake to cool in the pan for 10 minutes before transferring it to a wire rack to cool completely.
4. **Prepare the Blueberry Glaze (Optional):**
    - In a small bowl, whisk together the powdered sugar, blueberry juice, and lemon juice until smooth. Adjust the consistency with more juice or powdered sugar if needed.
    - Drizzle the glaze over the cooled cake.
5. **Prepare the Blueberry Frosting (Optional):**
    - In a large bowl, beat the butter and cream cheese together until creamy.
    - Gradually add the powdered sugar, beating until smooth.
    - Mix in the blueberry puree and vanilla extract until well combined. Adjust the consistency with more powdered sugar or blueberry puree if needed.
    - Frost the cooled cake with the blueberry frosting.
6. **Garnish and Serve:**
    - Optionally, garnish with fresh blueberries, a sprinkle of lemon zest, or mint leaves.
    - Slice and enjoy your homemade Blueberry Cake!

Tips:

- **Blueberry Distribution:** Tossing the blueberries in a bit of flour before folding them into the batter can help prevent them from sinking to the bottom of the cake.
- **Frozen Blueberries:** If using frozen blueberries, keep them frozen until just before folding into the batter to avoid bleeding into the cake batter.

Blueberry Cake offers a delicious burst of blueberry flavor in every bite, with a soft and moist texture that's sure to please. It's perfect for a summer dessert or as a sweet treat year-round.

Taro Cake

Ingredients:

For the Cake:

- 1 1/2 cups taro root (peeled and diced)
- 1 cup granulated sugar
- 1/2 cup unsalted butter, room temperature
- 2 large eggs
- 1 cup all-purpose flour
- 1/2 cup milk
- 1 tsp baking powder
- 1/2 tsp vanilla extract
- 1/4 tsp salt

For the Taro Frosting (Optional):

- 1/2 cup unsalted butter, room temperature
- 4 oz cream cheese, room temperature
- 1 cup taro puree (can be made by steaming and blending taro root)
- 2-3 cups powdered sugar
- 1/2 tsp vanilla extract

Optional Garnish:

- Toasted sesame seeds
- Fresh fruit (such as strawberries or mango slices)
- Shredded coconut

Instructions:

1. **Prepare the Taro:**
   - Peel and dice the taro root. Steam or boil until tender, about 15-20 minutes.
   - Mash the cooked taro until smooth or use a food processor to make a puree. Allow to cool.
2. **Preheat Oven:**
   - Preheat your oven to 350°F (175°C). Grease and flour an 8-inch round cake pan or line it with parchment paper.
3. **Prepare the Cake Batter:**
   - In a medium bowl, whisk together the flour, baking powder, and salt.
   - In a large bowl, cream together the butter and granulated sugar until light and fluffy.
   - Add the eggs one at a time, beating well after each addition. Mix in the vanilla extract.

- Gradually add the flour mixture to the butter mixture, alternating with the milk. Begin and end with the dry ingredients, mixing until just combined.
- Gently fold in the taro puree.

4. **Bake the Cake:**
    - Pour the batter into the prepared cake pan and smooth the top.
    - Bake for 30-35 minutes, or until a toothpick inserted into the center comes out clean.
    - Allow the cake to cool in the pan for 10 minutes before transferring it to a wire rack to cool completely.

5. **Prepare the Taro Frosting (Optional):**
    - In a large bowl, beat the butter and cream cheese together until creamy.
    - Gradually add the powdered sugar, beating until smooth.
    - Mix in the taro puree and vanilla extract until well combined. Adjust the consistency with more powdered sugar if needed.

6. **Assemble and Frost the Cake:**
    - Once the cake is completely cooled, place one layer on a serving plate or cake stand.
    - Spread a layer of taro frosting on top of the first layer.
    - Place the second cake layer on top and frost the top and sides of the cake with the remaining taro frosting.

7. **Garnish and Serve:**
    - Optionally, garnish with toasted sesame seeds, fresh fruit, or shredded coconut.
    - Slice and enjoy your homemade Taro Cake!

Tips:

- **Taro Puree:** If you want a smoother texture, ensure the taro is well-pureed and free of lumps before mixing it into the cake batter or frosting.
- **Flavor Adjustments:** Adjust the sweetness of the cake and frosting according to your taste by adding more or less sugar.

Taro Cake offers a delightful flavor and texture that's both comforting and exotic, making it a great choice for a unique dessert.

Dalgona Coffee Cake

Ingredients:

For the Cake:

- 1 1/2 cups all-purpose flour
- 1 cup granulated sugar
- 1/2 cup unsalted butter, room temperature
- 2 large eggs
- 1/2 cup milk
- 1 tsp vanilla extract
- 1 1/2 tsp baking powder
- 1/2 tsp baking soda
- 1/4 tsp salt

For the Dalgona Coffee Topping:

- 2 tbsp instant coffee granules
- 2 tbsp granulated sugar
- 2 tbsp hot water
- 1/2 cup heavy cream (for whipping)

Optional Garnish:

- Cocoa powder
- Coffee beans
- Whipped cream

Instructions:

1. **Preheat Oven:**
    - Preheat your oven to 350°F (175°C). Grease and flour an 8-inch round cake pan or line it with parchment paper.
2. **Prepare the Cake Batter:**
    - In a medium bowl, whisk together the flour, baking powder, baking soda, and salt.
    - In a large bowl, cream together the butter and granulated sugar until light and fluffy.
    - Add the eggs one at a time, beating well after each addition. Mix in the vanilla extract.
    - Gradually add the dry ingredients to the butter mixture, alternating with the milk. Begin and end with the dry ingredients, mixing until just combined.
3. **Bake the Cake:**
    - Pour the batter into the prepared cake pan and smooth the top.
    - Bake for 25-30 minutes, or until a toothpick inserted into the center comes out clean.

- Allow the cake to cool in the pan for 10 minutes before transferring it to a wire rack to cool completely.
4. **Prepare the Dalgona Coffee Topping:**
    - In a medium bowl, combine the instant coffee granules, granulated sugar, and hot water.
    - Use a hand mixer or stand mixer to beat the mixture until it becomes thick, fluffy, and forms stiff peaks. This may take a few minutes.
    - Gently fold in the heavy cream until well combined and fluffy. The mixture should be thick and spreadable.
5. **Assemble the Cake:**
    - Once the cake is completely cooled, spread a layer of Dalgona coffee topping over the top of the cake. You can use a spatula or the back of a spoon to create a smooth layer.
6. **Garnish and Serve:**
    - Optionally, garnish with a dusting of cocoa powder, coffee beans, or a dollop of whipped cream.
    - Slice and enjoy your Dalgona Coffee Cake!

Tips:

- **Consistency:** Ensure that the Dalgona coffee topping is thick enough to hold its shape. If it's too thin, it may not spread well on the cake.
- **Chilling:** If you're having trouble spreading the Dalgona topping, chill it briefly in the refrigerator to firm it up.

Dalgona Coffee Cake offers a fun and trendy twist on traditional cake recipes, combining the whipped coffee trend with a classic cake base for a delicious and eye-catching dessert.

Apple Cinnamon Cake

Ingredients:

For the Cake:

- 1 1/2 cups all-purpose flour
- 1 cup granulated sugar
- 1/2 cup unsalted butter, room temperature
- 2 large eggs
- 1/2 cup milk
- 1/2 tsp vanilla extract
- 1 1/2 tsp baking powder
- 1/2 tsp baking soda
- 1/4 tsp salt
- 1 tsp ground cinnamon
- 1 1/2 cups peeled and chopped apples (such as Granny Smith or Honeycrisp)
- 1/4 cup finely chopped nuts (optional, such as walnuts or pecans)

For the Cinnamon Sugar Topping:

- 1/4 cup granulated sugar
- 1 tsp ground cinnamon

For the Optional Glaze:

- 1/2 cup powdered sugar
- 1-2 tbsp milk or cream
- 1/2 tsp vanilla extract

Instructions:

1. **Preheat Oven:**
    - Preheat your oven to 350°F (175°C). Grease and flour an 8-inch round or square cake pan, or line it with parchment paper.
2. **Prepare the Cake Batter:**
    - In a medium bowl, whisk together the flour, baking powder, baking soda, salt, and ground cinnamon.
    - In a large bowl, cream together the butter and granulated sugar until light and fluffy.
    - Add the eggs one at a time, beating well after each addition. Mix in the vanilla extract.
    - Gradually add the dry ingredients to the butter mixture, alternating with the milk. Begin and end with the dry ingredients, mixing until just combined.
    - Gently fold in the chopped apples and nuts (if using).
3. **Prepare the Cinnamon Sugar Topping:**

- In a small bowl, mix together the granulated sugar and ground cinnamon.
4. **Bake the Cake:**
   - Pour the batter into the prepared cake pan and smooth the top.
   - Sprinkle the cinnamon sugar topping evenly over the batter.
   - Bake for 30-35 minutes, or until a toothpick inserted into the center comes out clean.
   - Allow the cake to cool in the pan for 10 minutes before transferring it to a wire rack to cool completely.
5. **Prepare the Optional Glaze (if using):**
   - In a small bowl, whisk together the powdered sugar, milk or cream, and vanilla extract until smooth.
   - Drizzle the glaze over the cooled cake.
6. **Serve and Enjoy:**
   - Slice and enjoy your Apple Cinnamon Cake. It's wonderful on its own or served with a scoop of vanilla ice cream or a dollop of whipped cream.

Tips:

- **Apple Choice:** Use apples that hold their shape well during baking for a better texture in the cake. Granny Smith and Honeycrisp are great choices.
- **Mixing Apples:** Tossing the chopped apples in a bit of flour before adding them to the batter can help prevent them from sinking to the bottom.

Apple Cinnamon Cake is a delightful and aromatic dessert that pairs perfectly with a cup of tea or coffee. Its combination of tender cake, sweet apples, and warm cinnamon makes it a comforting treat for any time of year.

Raspberry Cake

Ingredients:

For the Cake:

- 1 1/2 cups all-purpose flour
- 1 cup granulated sugar
- 1/2 cup unsalted butter, room temperature
- 2 large eggs
- 1/2 cup milk
- 1/2 cup fresh or frozen raspberries (if using frozen, do not thaw)
- 1 tsp vanilla extract
- 1 1/2 tsp baking powder
- 1/2 tsp baking soda
- 1/4 tsp salt

For the Raspberry Frosting (Optional):

- 1/2 cup unsalted butter, room temperature
- 4 oz cream cheese, room temperature
- 2 cups powdered sugar
- 1/4 cup raspberry puree (blend fresh or thawed raspberries)
- 1/2 tsp vanilla extract

For the Raspberry Sauce (Optional):

- 1 cup fresh or frozen raspberries
- 1/4 cup granulated sugar
- 1 tbsp lemon juice

Optional Garnish:

- Fresh raspberries
- Mint leaves
- Lemon zest

Instructions:

1. **Preheat Oven:**
   - Preheat your oven to 350°F (175°C). Grease and flour an 8-inch round cake pan or line it with parchment paper.
2. **Prepare the Cake Batter:**
   - In a medium bowl, whisk together the flour, baking powder, baking soda, and salt.
   - In a large bowl, cream together the butter and granulated sugar until light and fluffy.

- Add the eggs one at a time, beating well after each addition. Mix in the vanilla extract.
- Gradually add the dry ingredients to the butter mixture, alternating with the milk. Begin and end with the dry ingredients, mixing until just combined.
- Gently fold in the raspberries. If using frozen raspberries, toss them in a bit of flour before adding to the batter to help prevent them from sinking.

3. **Bake the Cake:**
   - Pour the batter into the prepared cake pan and smooth the top.
   - Bake for 25-30 minutes, or until a toothpick inserted into the center comes out clean.
   - Allow the cake to cool in the pan for 10 minutes before transferring it to a wire rack to cool completely.

4. **Prepare the Raspberry Frosting (Optional):**
   - In a large bowl, beat the butter and cream cheese together until creamy and smooth.
   - Gradually add the powdered sugar, beating until well combined.
   - Mix in the raspberry puree and vanilla extract until smooth.

5. **Prepare the Raspberry Sauce (Optional):**
   - In a small saucepan, combine the raspberries, sugar, and lemon juice.
   - Cook over medium heat, stirring frequently, until the raspberries break down and the sauce thickens, about 5-7 minutes.
   - Strain through a fine mesh sieve to remove seeds, if desired. Let cool.

6. **Assemble and Garnish the Cake:**
   - Once the cake is completely cooled, spread the raspberry frosting over the top and sides of the cake, if using.
   - Drizzle with raspberry sauce if desired.
   - Garnish with fresh raspberries, mint leaves, or lemon zest if desired.

7. **Serve and Enjoy:**
   - Slice and enjoy your Raspberry Cake!

Tips:

- **Raspberry Puree:** To make raspberry puree, simply blend fresh or thawed raspberries until smooth. You can strain it if you want a seedless puree.
- **Flavor Enhancements:** For an extra burst of flavor, consider adding a splash of lemon juice or zest to the cake batter.

Raspberry Cake is a deliciously fruity and elegant dessert that's perfect for a special occasion or a sweet treat any day of the week. The combination of tangy raspberries and soft cake makes for a delightful experience with each bite.

Walnut Cake

Ingredients:

For the Cake:

- 1 1/2 cups all-purpose flour
- 1 cup granulated sugar
- 1/2 cup unsalted butter, room temperature
- 2 large eggs
- 1/2 cup milk
- 1 tsp vanilla extract
- 1 tsp baking powder
- 1/2 tsp baking soda
- 1/4 tsp salt
- 1 cup chopped walnuts (lightly toasted if desired)

For the Walnut Frosting (Optional):

- 1/2 cup unsalted butter, room temperature
- 4 oz cream cheese, room temperature
- 2 cups powdered sugar
- 1/2 cup finely chopped walnuts
- 1/2 tsp vanilla extract

Optional Garnish:

- Whole walnuts
- Caramel sauce
- Extra chopped walnuts

Instructions:

1. **Preheat Oven:**
    - Preheat your oven to 350°F (175°C). Grease and flour an 8-inch round or square cake pan, or line it with parchment paper.
2. **Prepare the Cake Batter:**
    - In a medium bowl, whisk together the flour, baking powder, baking soda, and salt.
    - In a large bowl, cream together the butter and granulated sugar until light and fluffy.
    - Add the eggs one at a time, beating well after each addition. Mix in the vanilla extract.
    - Gradually add the dry ingredients to the butter mixture, alternating with the milk. Begin and end with the dry ingredients, mixing until just combined.
    - Gently fold in the chopped walnuts.
3. **Bake the Cake:**

- Pour the batter into the prepared cake pan and smooth the top.
- Bake for 25-30 minutes, or until a toothpick inserted into the center comes out clean.
- Allow the cake to cool in the pan for 10 minutes before transferring it to a wire rack to cool completely.
4. **Prepare the Walnut Frosting (Optional):**
    - In a large bowl, beat the butter and cream cheese together until creamy and smooth.
    - Gradually add the powdered sugar, beating until well combined.
    - Mix in the finely chopped walnuts and vanilla extract until smooth.
5. **Assemble and Garnish the Cake:**
    - Once the cake is completely cooled, spread the walnut frosting over the top and sides of the cake, if using.
    - Garnish with whole walnuts or additional chopped walnuts, and drizzle with caramel sauce if desired.
6. **Serve and Enjoy:**
    - Slice and enjoy your Walnut Cake!

Tips:

- **Toasting Walnuts:** Lightly toasting the walnuts enhances their flavor and adds a bit of crunch. Simply toast them in a dry skillet over medium heat until fragrant, stirring frequently.
- **Texture:** For a more textured cake, you can chop the walnuts coarsely. If you prefer a smoother texture, finely chop them or use walnut meal.

Walnut Cake is a delightful dessert that offers a rich, nutty flavor with a tender crumb. Whether you enjoy it plain or with frosting, it's a comforting treat perfect for any occasion.

Pear Cake

Ingredients:

For the Cake:

- 1 1/2 cups all-purpose flour
- 1 cup granulated sugar
- 1/2 cup unsalted butter, room temperature
- 2 large eggs
- 1/2 cup milk
- 1 tsp vanilla extract
- 1 1/2 tsp baking powder
- 1/2 tsp baking soda
- 1/4 tsp salt
- 2 cups peeled and chopped pears (about 2 medium pears, such as Bartlett or Bosc)

For the Optional Cinnamon Sugar Topping:

- 1/4 cup granulated sugar
- 1 tsp ground cinnamon

For the Optional Glaze:

- 1/2 cup powdered sugar
- 2-3 tbsp milk or cream
- 1/2 tsp vanilla extract

Optional Garnish:

- Fresh pear slices
- A dusting of powdered sugar

Instructions:

1. **Preheat Oven:**
    - Preheat your oven to 350°F (175°C). Grease and flour an 8-inch round or square cake pan, or line it with parchment paper.
2. **Prepare the Cake Batter:**
    - In a medium bowl, whisk together the flour, baking powder, baking soda, and salt.
    - In a large bowl, cream together the butter and granulated sugar until light and fluffy.
    - Add the eggs one at a time, beating well after each addition. Mix in the vanilla extract.
    - Gradually add the dry ingredients to the butter mixture, alternating with the milk. Begin and end with the dry ingredients, mixing until just combined.

- Fold in the chopped pears gently.
3. **Prepare the Cinnamon Sugar Topping (Optional):**
   - In a small bowl, mix together the granulated sugar and ground cinnamon.
   - Sprinkle the mixture evenly over the batter in the cake pan for a spiced, crunchy top.
4. **Bake the Cake:**
   - Pour the batter into the prepared cake pan and smooth the top.
   - Bake for 35-40 minutes, or until a toothpick inserted into the center comes out clean.
   - Allow the cake to cool in the pan for 10 minutes before transferring it to a wire rack to cool completely.
5. **Prepare the Glaze (Optional):**
   - In a small bowl, whisk together the powdered sugar, milk or cream, and vanilla extract until smooth.
   - Drizzle the glaze over the cooled cake.
6. **Garnish and Serve:**
   - Optionally, garnish with fresh pear slices or a light dusting of powdered sugar.
   - Slice and enjoy your Pear Cake!

Tips:

- **Pears:** Use ripe but firm pears for the best texture. Overripe pears can become mushy during baking.
- **Flour Tossing:** Toss the chopped pears in a bit of flour before adding them to the batter to help them distribute evenly and prevent sinking.

Pear Cake is a delightful dessert that highlights the natural sweetness and flavor of pears. It's perfect for a cozy afternoon treat or as a simple yet elegant dessert for gatherings.

Chocolate Green Tea Cake

Ingredients:

For the Cake:

- 1 cup all-purpose flour
- 1/2 cup unsweetened cocoa powder
- 1 cup granulated sugar
- 1/2 cup unsalted butter, room temperature
- 2 large eggs
- 1/2 cup milk
- 1/2 cup boiling water
- 1/4 cup green tea powder (matcha)
- 1 1/2 tsp baking powder
- 1/2 tsp baking soda
- 1/4 tsp salt
- 1 tsp vanilla extract

For the Matcha Glaze (Optional):

- 1 cup powdered sugar
- 2-3 tbsp milk or cream
- 1-2 tbsp green tea powder (matcha)
- 1/2 tsp vanilla extract

For the Chocolate Ganache (Optional):

- 1/2 cup heavy cream
- 4 oz semisweet chocolate, chopped

Optional Garnish:

- Additional matcha powder for dusting
- Fresh berries or mint leaves

Instructions:

1. **Preheat Oven:**
   - Preheat your oven to 350°F (175°C). Grease and flour an 8-inch round cake pan, or line it with parchment paper.
2. **Prepare the Cake Batter:**
   - In a medium bowl, whisk together the flour, cocoa powder, baking powder, baking soda, and salt.
   - In a large bowl, cream together the butter and granulated sugar until light and fluffy.

- Add the eggs one at a time, beating well after each addition. Mix in the vanilla extract.
- Gradually add the dry ingredients to the butter mixture, alternating with the milk. Begin and end with the dry ingredients, mixing until just combined.
- Stir in the green tea powder (matcha) until well combined.
- Fold in the boiling water carefully; the batter will be thin but this helps to create a moist cake.

3. **Bake the Cake:**
    - Pour the batter into the prepared cake pan and smooth the top.
    - Bake for 30-35 minutes, or until a toothpick inserted into the center comes out clean.
    - Allow the cake to cool in the pan for 10 minutes before transferring it to a wire rack to cool completely.

4. **Prepare the Matcha Glaze (Optional):**
    - In a small bowl, whisk together the powdered sugar, green tea powder, vanilla extract, and milk or cream until smooth. Adjust the consistency with more milk or powdered sugar if needed.
    - Drizzle over the cooled cake.

5. **Prepare the Chocolate Ganache (Optional):**
    - In a small saucepan, heat the heavy cream until just beginning to simmer.
    - Pour the hot cream over the chopped chocolate in a heatproof bowl. Let sit for 2-3 minutes, then stir until smooth and glossy.
    - Allow the ganache to cool slightly before spreading or drizzling over the cake.

6. **Garnish and Serve:**
    - Optionally, dust with additional matcha powder, and garnish with fresh berries or mint leaves.
    - Slice and enjoy your Chocolate Green Tea Cake!

Tips:

- **Matcha Quality:** Use high-quality culinary matcha for the best flavor and color.
- **Ganache:** If the ganache is too thick, you can gently reheat it until it reaches the desired consistency. If too thin, let it cool a bit more to thicken.

Chocolate Green Tea Cake offers a delightful contrast of flavors and a beautiful appearance. It's perfect for impressing guests or treating yourself to something special.

Sweet Red Bean Paste Cake

Ingredients:

For the Cake:

- 1 cup all-purpose flour
- 1/2 cup granulated sugar
- 1/2 cup unsweetened red bean paste (available at Asian grocery stores)
- 1/2 cup unsalted butter, room temperature
- 2 large eggs
- 1/2 cup milk
- 1 tsp baking powder
- 1/2 tsp vanilla extract
- 1/4 tsp salt

For the Red Bean Filling (Optional):

- 1/2 cup sweetened red bean paste (if you want to add a filling)

For Garnish (Optional):

- Powdered sugar
- Sesame seeds

Instructions:

1. **Preheat Oven:**
    - Preheat your oven to 350°F (175°C). Grease and flour an 8-inch round or square cake pan, or line it with parchment paper.
2. **Prepare the Cake Batter:**
    - In a medium bowl, whisk together the flour, baking powder, and salt.
    - In a large bowl, cream together the butter and granulated sugar until light and fluffy.
    - Add the eggs one at a time, beating well after each addition. Mix in the vanilla extract.
    - Gradually add the dry ingredients to the butter mixture, alternating with the milk. Begin and end with the dry ingredients, mixing until just combined.
    - Gently fold in the red bean paste until evenly distributed.
3. **Add Red Bean Filling (Optional):**
    - If using a red bean filling, spoon half of the batter into the prepared cake pan.
    - Dot the surface with spoonfuls of sweetened red bean paste.
    - Top with the remaining batter and smooth the top.
4. **Bake the Cake:**
    - Bake for 30-35 minutes, or until a toothpick inserted into the center comes out clean.

- Allow the cake to cool in the pan for 10 minutes before transferring it to a wire rack to cool completely.
5. **Garnish and Serve:**
    - Optionally, dust with powdered sugar or sprinkle with sesame seeds before serving.
    - Slice and enjoy your Sweet Red Bean Paste Cake!

Tips:

- **Red Bean Paste:** You can find sweetened red bean paste in Asian grocery stores or online. If making your own, cook adzuki beans with sugar until they form a paste.
- **Texture:** For a smoother texture, ensure the red bean paste is well incorporated into the batter, or use it as a filling for added texture.

Sweet Red Bean Paste Cake is a unique and flavorful dessert that combines the richness of red bean paste with the lightness of a cake. It's a great way to enjoy traditional flavors in a modern cake format.

Carrot Cake

Ingredients:

For the Cake:

- 1 1/2 cups all-purpose flour
- 1 cup granulated sugar
- 1/2 cup packed brown sugar
- 1 tsp baking powder
- 1/2 tsp baking soda
- 1/2 tsp salt
- 1 tsp ground cinnamon
- 1/2 tsp ground ginger
- 1/4 tsp ground nutmeg
- 1/2 cup vegetable oil
- 3 large eggs
- 2 cups finely grated carrots (about 4 medium carrots)
- 1/2 cup crushed pineapple, drained
- 1/2 cup chopped walnuts or pecans (optional)
- 1/4 cup shredded coconut (optional)
- 1 tsp vanilla extract

For the Cream Cheese Frosting:

- 8 oz cream cheese, room temperature
- 1/2 cup unsalted butter, room temperature
- 3-4 cups powdered sugar (adjust for desired sweetness)
- 1 tsp vanilla extract

Optional Garnish:

- Additional chopped nuts
- Shredded coconut
- Carrot decorations

Instructions:

1. **Preheat Oven:**
   - Preheat your oven to 350°F (175°C). Grease and flour two 8-inch round cake pans or line them with parchment paper.
2. **Prepare the Cake Batter:**
   - In a large bowl, whisk together the flour, granulated sugar, brown sugar, baking powder, baking soda, salt, cinnamon, ginger, and nutmeg.
   - In another bowl, whisk together the oil, eggs, and vanilla extract.

- Gradually add the wet ingredients to the dry ingredients, mixing until just combined.
- Fold in the grated carrots, crushed pineapple, chopped nuts (if using), and shredded coconut (if using).

3. **Bake the Cake:**
   - Divide the batter evenly between the prepared cake pans and smooth the tops.
   - Bake for 25-30 minutes, or until a toothpick inserted into the center comes out clean.
   - Allow the cakes to cool in the pans for 10 minutes before transferring them to a wire rack to cool completely.
4. **Prepare the Cream Cheese Frosting:**
   - In a large bowl, beat the cream cheese and butter together until creamy and smooth.
   - Gradually add the powdered sugar, beating until well combined and fluffy.
   - Mix in the vanilla extract.
5. **Assemble and Frost the Cake:**
   - Once the cakes are completely cooled, spread a layer of cream cheese frosting on top of one cake layer.
   - Place the second cake layer on top and frost the top and sides of the cake with the remaining cream cheese frosting.
   - Optionally, garnish with additional chopped nuts, shredded coconut, or carrot decorations.
6. **Serve and Enjoy:**
   - Slice and enjoy your Carrot Cake!

Tips:

- **Carrot Grating:** For the best texture, grate the carrots finely. Large chunks of carrot can affect the cake's consistency.
- **Moisture Control:** Ensure the pineapple is well-drained to prevent excess moisture in the batter.
- **Storage:** Store leftover cake in an airtight container in the refrigerator for up to a week.

Carrot Cake is a comforting and flavorful dessert that's perfect for any occasion, from everyday treats to special celebrations. The combination of spiced cake and creamy frosting makes it a perennial favorite.

Milk Cake

Ingredients:

- 2 cups whole milk
- 1/2 cup sugar
- 1/4 cup milk powder
- 2 tbsp ghee (clarified butter)
- 1/4 cup water
- 1/2 tsp cardamom powder
- 1/4 cup chopped nuts (such as almonds, cashews, or pistachios)
- 1 tbsp chopped dried fruits (such as raisins or dates, optional)

Instructions:

1. **Prepare the Milk Mixture:**
   - In a heavy-bottomed pan, heat the ghee over medium heat.
   - Add the whole milk to the pan and bring it to a boil, stirring continuously to prevent it from scorching.
2. **Cook the Milk:**
   - Once the milk comes to a boil, reduce the heat to low and let it simmer, stirring frequently, until it reduces by about half. This may take around 10-15 minutes.
3. **Add Sugar and Milk Powder:**
   - Stir in the sugar and continue to cook, allowing it to dissolve completely.
   - Add the milk powder and mix well. Cook the mixture over low heat, stirring constantly, until it thickens and starts to leave the sides of the pan. This should take another 5-10 minutes.
4. **Flavor the Mixture:**
   - Add the cardamom powder and mix well.
   - If using, add the chopped dried fruits at this stage.
5. **Set the Milk Cake:**
   - Transfer the mixture to a greased plate or tray. Use a spatula to spread it evenly and smooth the surface.
   - Allow it to cool slightly. Once it starts to set but is still warm, cut it into pieces or shapes of your choice.
6. **Garnish and Cool:**
   - Garnish with chopped nuts while still warm.
   - Let the Milk Cake cool completely before serving. It will firm up as it cools.
7. **Serve and Enjoy:**
   - Enjoy your Milk Cake as a delicious dessert or sweet treat!

Tips:

- **Milk Reduction:** Ensure that you cook the milk on low heat and stir frequently to prevent it from burning.

- **Consistency:** The mixture should reach a fudge-like consistency before you transfer it to the plate. It should hold together but not be too dry.

Milk Cake is a rich, indulgent treat that's perfect for celebrations and special occasions. Its creamy texture and aromatic flavor make it a favorite among sweet lovers.

Soybean Cake

Ingredients:

For the Soybean Mixture:

- 1 cup dried soybeans
- 3 cups water (for soaking)
- 3 cups water (for blending)

For the Cake:

- 1/2 cup granulated sugar (adjust to taste)
- 1/4 cup cornstarch
- 1/4 cup water (for cornstarch slurry)
- 1/4 tsp vanilla extract (optional)

For Garnish (Optional):

- Sweet red bean paste
- Fresh fruit (such as berries or sliced peaches)
- Honey or maple syrup

Instructions:

1. **Soak the Soybeans:**
    - Rinse the dried soybeans and soak them in 3 cups of water overnight or for at least 8 hours.
2. **Prepare the Soybean Mixture:**
    - Drain and rinse the soaked soybeans.
    - In a blender, combine the soybeans with 3 cups of fresh water. Blend until smooth and creamy.
3. **Extract Soy Milk:**
    - Line a large bowl with a cheesecloth or a nut milk bag.
    - Pour the blended soybean mixture into the lined bowl.
    - Gather the edges of the cheesecloth and twist to squeeze out the soy milk into the bowl. The soy milk should be smooth and free of solids.
4. **Cook the Soy Milk:**
    - Transfer the soy milk to a saucepan and heat it over medium heat. Bring it to a gentle boil, stirring frequently to prevent scorching. Reduce the heat and simmer for 5 minutes.
5. **Prepare the Cornstarch Slurry:**
    - In a small bowl, mix the cornstarch with 1/4 cup water until smooth.
6. **Thicken the Soy Milk:**
    - Slowly pour the cornstarch slurry into the hot soy milk while stirring continuously.

- Continue to cook and stir until the mixture thickens and reaches a pudding-like consistency.
7. **Add Sugar and Flavor:**
    - Stir in the granulated sugar and vanilla extract (if using). Mix well until the sugar is fully dissolved.
8. **Set the Soybean Cake:**
    - Pour the thickened soy milk mixture into a greased or parchment-lined dish or cake pan.
    - Smooth the top with a spatula.
    - Allow it to cool to room temperature, then refrigerate for at least 2 hours to set completely.
9. **Serve and Garnish:**
    - Once set, cut the Soybean Cake into squares or slices.
    - Optionally, top with sweet red bean paste, fresh fruit, or a drizzle of honey or maple syrup.
10. **Enjoy:**
    - Serve chilled or at room temperature as a refreshing dessert or snack.

Tips:

- **Texture:** The texture of the Soybean Cake should be smooth and creamy. If you prefer a firmer texture, you can increase the amount of cornstarch slightly.
- **Flavor Variations:** You can experiment with adding different flavorings, such as matcha powder or cocoa powder, to the soy milk mixture before thickening.

Soybean Cake is a versatile and healthy dessert that's easy to make and can be customized to your taste preferences. Enjoy its subtle, nutty flavor with a variety of toppings and garnishes!

Cherry Blossom Cake

Ingredients:

For the Cake:

- 1 1/2 cups all-purpose flour
- 1 cup granulated sugar
- 1/2 cup unsalted butter, room temperature
- 2 large eggs
- 1/2 cup milk
- 1/4 cup almond flour
- 1/2 tsp baking powder
- 1/2 tsp baking soda
- 1/4 tsp salt
- 1/2 tsp almond extract
- 1/4 tsp rose water (optional, for a subtle floral flavor)
- 1 cup fresh or frozen cherries, pitted and chopped

For the Cherry Blossom Buttercream:

- 1 cup unsalted butter, room temperature
- 3-4 cups powdered sugar
- 2 tbsp cherry preserves or cherry jam
- 1-2 tbsp milk or cream (adjust for consistency)
- 1/4 tsp almond extract
- A few drops of red or pink food coloring (optional, for a cherry blossom color)

For Garnish:

- Edible cherry blossoms or cherry blossom petals (if available)
- Fresh cherries
- A dusting of powdered sugar

Instructions:

1. **Preheat Oven:**
   - Preheat your oven to 350°F (175°C). Grease and flour two 8-inch round cake pans, or line them with parchment paper.
2. **Prepare the Cake Batter:**
   - In a medium bowl, whisk together the flour, baking powder, baking soda, salt, and almond flour.
   - In a large bowl, cream together the butter and granulated sugar until light and fluffy.
   - Add the eggs one at a time, beating well after each addition. Mix in the almond extract and rose water (if using).

- Gradually add the dry ingredients to the butter mixture, alternating with the milk. Begin and end with the dry ingredients, mixing until just combined.
- Gently fold in the chopped cherries.
3. **Bake the Cake:**
    - Divide the batter evenly between the prepared cake pans and smooth the tops.
    - Bake for 25-30 minutes, or until a toothpick inserted into the center comes out clean.
    - Allow the cakes to cool in the pans for 10 minutes before transferring them to a wire rack to cool completely.
4. **Prepare the Cherry Blossom Buttercream:**
    - In a large bowl, beat the butter until creamy and smooth.
    - Gradually add the powdered sugar, beating until well combined and fluffy.
    - Mix in the cherry preserves or jam and almond extract.
    - Add milk or cream as needed to achieve a spreadable consistency.
    - If desired, add a few drops of red or pink food coloring to achieve a light pink color, resembling cherry blossoms.
5. **Assemble and Frost the Cake:**
    - Once the cakes are completely cooled, spread a layer of buttercream on top of one cake layer.
    - Place the second cake layer on top and frost the top and sides of the cake with the remaining buttercream.
6. **Garnish and Serve:**
    - Garnish with edible cherry blossoms or cherry blossom petals, fresh cherries, and a dusting of powdered sugar.
    - Slice and enjoy your Cherry Blossom Cake!

Tips:

- **Cherry Prep:** If using frozen cherries, thaw and drain them well to avoid excess moisture in the cake batter.
- **Rose Water:** Rose water adds a subtle floral note. If you prefer a more pronounced floral flavor, you can adjust the amount according to taste.
- **Edible Blossoms:** If you can't find edible cherry blossoms, you can use other edible flowers or simply garnish with fresh cherries.

Cherry Blossom Cake is a delightful and visually appealing dessert that captures the essence of cherry blossom season. Its delicate flavors and elegant presentation make it a perfect choice for special occasions and celebrations.

Fig Cake

Ingredients:

For the Cake:

- 1 1/2 cups dried figs (or fresh figs if in season)
- 1 cup boiling water
- 1/2 cup unsalted butter, room temperature
- 1 cup granulated sugar
- 1/2 cup packed brown sugar
- 2 large eggs
- 1 1/2 cups all-purpose flour
- 1 tsp baking powder
- 1/2 tsp baking soda
- 1/4 tsp salt
- 1 tsp ground cinnamon
- 1/4 tsp ground nutmeg
- 1/4 tsp ground cloves (optional)
- 1/2 cup chopped walnuts or pecans (optional)
- 1/2 cup buttermilk or sour cream
- 1 tsp vanilla extract

For the Cream Cheese Frosting (optional):

- 8 oz cream cheese, room temperature
- 1/2 cup unsalted butter, room temperature
- 3-4 cups powdered sugar
- 1 tsp vanilla extract

Optional Garnish:

- Additional chopped nuts
- Fresh fig slices

Instructions:

1. **Prepare the Figs:**
   - If using dried figs, chop them into small pieces. Place them in a bowl and pour the boiling water over them. Let soak for 15-20 minutes to soften.
   - Drain the figs and chop them further if needed. If using fresh figs, wash, remove stems, and chop them into small pieces.
2. **Preheat Oven:**
   - Preheat your oven to 350°F (175°C). Grease and flour two 8-inch round cake pans or line them with parchment paper.
3. **Prepare the Cake Batter:**

- In a medium bowl, whisk together the flour, baking powder, baking soda, salt, cinnamon, nutmeg, and cloves (if using).
  - In a large bowl, cream together the butter, granulated sugar, and brown sugar until light and fluffy.
  - Add the eggs one at a time, beating well after each addition.
  - Mix in the vanilla extract.
  - Gradually add the dry ingredients to the butter mixture, alternating with the buttermilk or sour cream. Begin and end with the dry ingredients, mixing until just combined.
  - Fold in the chopped figs and nuts (if using).
4. **Bake the Cake:**
   - Divide the batter evenly between the prepared cake pans and smooth the tops.
   - Bake for 25-30 minutes, or until a toothpick inserted into the center comes out clean.
   - Allow the cakes to cool in the pans for 10 minutes before transferring them to a wire rack to cool completely.
5. **Prepare the Cream Cheese Frosting (Optional):**
   - In a large bowl, beat the cream cheese and butter together until creamy and smooth.
   - Gradually add the powdered sugar, beating until well combined and fluffy.
   - Mix in the vanilla extract.
6. **Assemble and Frost the Cake:**
   - Once the cakes are completely cooled, spread a layer of cream cheese frosting on top of one cake layer.
   - Place the second cake layer on top and frost the top and sides of the cake with the remaining frosting.
   - Optionally, garnish with additional chopped nuts and fresh fig slices.
7. **Serve and Enjoy:**
   - Slice and enjoy your Fig Cake!

Tips:

- **Figs:** For the best flavor, use ripe figs if they're in season. Dried figs are a good alternative and provide a concentrated sweetness.
- **Texture:** Be sure not to overmix the batter after adding the figs to maintain a tender cake crumb.
- **Storage:** Store the cake in an airtight container at room temperature for up to 3 days or refrigerate for longer shelf life.

Fig Cake is a delightful and moist dessert that showcases the natural sweetness of figs, enhanced with warm spices and optionally topped with creamy frosting. It's perfect for special occasions or as a comforting treat.

Hazelnut Cake

Ingredients:

For the Cake:

- 1 cup hazelnuts, toasted and skins removed
- 1 1/2 cups all-purpose flour
- 1 cup granulated sugar
- 1/2 cup unsalted butter, room temperature
- 2 large eggs
- 1/2 cup milk
- 1/4 cup hazelnut flour (or additional finely ground hazelnuts)
- 1 1/2 tsp baking powder
- 1/2 tsp baking soda
- 1/4 tsp salt
- 1 tsp vanilla extract

For the Hazelnut Frosting (Optional):

- 1 cup unsalted butter, room temperature
- 3-4 cups powdered sugar
- 1/2 cup hazelnut spread (such as Nutella)
- 1-2 tbsp milk or cream (adjust for consistency)
- 1 tsp vanilla extract

Optional Garnish:

- Chopped toasted hazelnuts
- Chocolate shavings or ganache

Instructions:

1. **Prepare the Hazelnuts:**
    - Preheat your oven to 350°F (175°C).
    - Spread the hazelnuts on a baking sheet and toast in the oven for 8-10 minutes, or until fragrant and the skins are slightly cracked.
    - Remove from the oven and let cool. Rub the hazelnuts between your hands or in a clean towel to remove the skins. Grind the nuts in a food processor until finely ground.
2. **Preheat Oven:**
    - Grease and flour two 8-inch round cake pans, or line them with parchment paper.
3. **Prepare the Cake Batter:**
    - In a medium bowl, whisk together the flour, hazelnut flour (or additional ground hazelnuts), baking powder, baking soda, and salt.

- In a large bowl, cream together the butter and granulated sugar until light and fluffy.
- Add the eggs one at a time, beating well after each addition.
- Mix in the vanilla extract.
- Gradually add the dry ingredients to the butter mixture, alternating with the milk. Begin and end with the dry ingredients, mixing until just combined.

4. **Bake the Cake:**
   - Divide the batter evenly between the prepared cake pans and smooth the tops.
   - Bake for 25-30 minutes, or until a toothpick inserted into the center comes out clean.
   - Allow the cakes to cool in the pans for 10 minutes before transferring them to a wire rack to cool completely.

5. **Prepare the Hazelnut Frosting (Optional):**
   - In a large bowl, beat the butter until creamy and smooth.
   - Gradually add the powdered sugar, beating until well combined and fluffy.
   - Mix in the hazelnut spread and vanilla extract.
   - Add milk or cream as needed to achieve a smooth, spreadable consistency.

6. **Assemble and Frost the Cake:**
   - Once the cakes are completely cooled, spread a layer of frosting on top of one cake layer.
   - Place the second cake layer on top and frost the top and sides of the cake with the remaining frosting.

7. **Garnish and Serve:**
   - Garnish with chopped toasted hazelnuts and chocolate shavings or ganache, if desired.
   - Slice and enjoy your Hazelnut Cake!

Tips:

- **Hazelnuts:** Ensure the hazelnuts are finely ground to avoid a gritty texture in the cake. Using a food processor is the best way to achieve this.
- **Consistency:** If the frosting is too thick, add a little more milk or cream. If it's too thin, add more powdered sugar.
- **Flavor Variations:** For a chocolate-hazelnut twist, consider adding cocoa powder to the cake batter or using chocolate ganache as a topping.

Hazelnut Cake is a delightful dessert that combines the rich, nutty flavor of hazelnuts with a tender, moist crumb. Whether enjoyed plain or with frosting, it's a treat that's sure to satisfy!

Apricot Cake

Ingredients:

For the Cake:

- 1 cup fresh apricots, pitted and chopped (or 1 cup dried apricots, chopped)
- 1 cup granulated sugar
- 1/2 cup unsalted butter, room temperature
- 2 large eggs
- 1 1/2 cups all-purpose flour
- 1/2 tsp baking powder
- 1/2 tsp baking soda
- 1/4 tsp salt
- 1/2 tsp ground cinnamon (optional)
- 1/2 cup buttermilk or sour cream
- 1 tsp vanilla extract

For the Apricot Glaze (Optional):

- 1/4 cup apricot preserves or jam
- 1 tbsp water

For Garnish (Optional):

- Sliced fresh apricots
- Powdered sugar

Instructions:

1. **Prepare the Apricots:**
    - If using fresh apricots, wash, pit, and chop them into small pieces. If using dried apricots, chop them into small pieces and, if desired, soak them in warm water for about 15 minutes to soften before draining.
2. **Preheat Oven:**
    - Preheat your oven to 350°F (175°C). Grease and flour a 9-inch round cake pan or line it with parchment paper.
3. **Prepare the Cake Batter:**
    - In a medium bowl, whisk together the flour, baking powder, baking soda, salt, and cinnamon (if using).
    - In a large bowl, cream together the butter and granulated sugar until light and fluffy.
    - Add the eggs one at a time, beating well after each addition.
    - Mix in the vanilla extract.

- Gradually add the dry ingredients to the butter mixture, alternating with the buttermilk or sour cream. Begin and end with the dry ingredients, mixing until just combined.
- Fold in the chopped apricots.
4. **Bake the Cake:**
    - Pour the batter into the prepared cake pan and smooth the top.
    - Bake for 30-35 minutes, or until a toothpick inserted into the center comes out clean.
    - Allow the cake to cool in the pan for 10 minutes before transferring it to a wire rack to cool completely.
5. **Prepare the Apricot Glaze (Optional):**
    - In a small saucepan, combine the apricot preserves and water.
    - Heat over low heat, stirring until the mixture is smooth and slightly thin.
    - Brush the glaze over the cooled cake for a shiny finish.
6. **Garnish and Serve:**
    - Garnish with fresh apricot slices and a dusting of powdered sugar, if desired.
    - Slice and enjoy your Apricot Cake!

Tips:

- **Dried Apricots:** If using dried apricots, soaking them can help rehydrate and plump them up, which adds moisture to the cake.
- **Texture:** For a smoother batter, make sure to chop the apricots into small, even pieces so they distribute evenly throughout the cake.
- **Storage:** Store the cake in an airtight container at room temperature for up to 3 days, or refrigerate for longer shelf life.

Apricot Cake is a versatile and flavorful dessert that beautifully showcases the sweet and tangy taste of apricots. Whether you enjoy it plain or with a glaze and garnish, it's a delightful treat for any occasion!

Pineapple Cake

Ingredients:

For the Cake:

- 1 cup crushed pineapple (canned or fresh), drained
- 1 1/2 cups all-purpose flour
- 1 cup granulated sugar
- 1/2 cup unsalted butter, room temperature
- 2 large eggs
- 1/2 cup buttermilk or sour cream
- 1 1/2 tsp baking powder
- 1/2 tsp baking soda
- 1/4 tsp salt
- 1/2 tsp vanilla extract
- 1/2 cup shredded coconut (optional)
- 1/2 cup chopped nuts (such as walnuts or pecans, optional)

For the Pineapple Glaze (Optional):

- 1/4 cup pineapple juice
- 1/4 cup granulated sugar
- 1 tbsp cornstarch

For the Cream Cheese Frosting (Optional):

- 8 oz cream cheese, room temperature
- 1/2 cup unsalted butter, room temperature
- 3-4 cups powdered sugar
- 1 tsp vanilla extract

Optional Garnish:

- Toasted coconut flakes
- Fresh pineapple slices or maraschino cherries

Instructions:

1. **Prepare the Pineapple:**
    - If using canned pineapple, drain it well and pat dry with paper towels to remove excess moisture. If using fresh pineapple, crush and drain it similarly.
2. **Preheat Oven:**
    - Preheat your oven to 350°F (175°C). Grease and flour a 9-inch round cake pan or line it with parchment paper.
3. **Prepare the Cake Batter:**

- In a medium bowl, whisk together the flour, baking powder, baking soda, and salt.
    - In a large bowl, cream together the butter and granulated sugar until light and fluffy.
    - Add the eggs one at a time, beating well after each addition.
    - Mix in the vanilla extract.
    - Gradually add the dry ingredients to the butter mixture, alternating with the buttermilk or sour cream. Begin and end with the dry ingredients, mixing until just combined.
    - Fold in the crushed pineapple, shredded coconut (if using), and chopped nuts (if using).
4. **Bake the Cake:**
    - Pour the batter into the prepared cake pan and smooth the top.
    - Bake for 30-35 minutes, or until a toothpick inserted into the center comes out clean.
    - Allow the cake to cool in the pan for 10 minutes before transferring it to a wire rack to cool completely.
5. **Prepare the Pineapple Glaze (Optional):**
    - In a small saucepan, combine the pineapple juice and granulated sugar.
    - Stir in the cornstarch.
    - Heat over medium heat, stirring constantly until the mixture thickens and becomes clear.
    - Brush the glaze over the cooled cake for a shiny finish.
6. **Prepare the Cream Cheese Frosting (Optional):**
    - In a large bowl, beat the cream cheese and butter together until creamy and smooth.
    - Gradually add the powdered sugar, beating until well combined and fluffy.
    - Mix in the vanilla extract.
7. **Assemble and Frost the Cake:**
    - Once the cake is completely cooled, spread a layer of cream cheese frosting on top of one cake layer if using.
    - Place the second cake layer on top and frost the top and sides of the cake with the remaining frosting.
8. **Garnish and Serve:**
    - Garnish with toasted coconut flakes and fresh pineapple slices or maraschino cherries, if desired.
    - Slice and enjoy your Pineapple Cake!

Tips:

- **Drain Pineapple:** Properly draining the pineapple is crucial to avoid excess moisture, which can make the cake soggy.
- **Texture:** The addition of coconut and nuts adds texture and flavor but can be omitted if you prefer a simpler cake.

- **Storage:** Store the cake in an airtight container at room temperature for up to 3 days, or refrigerate for longer shelf life.

Pineapple Cake is a tropical treat that brings a taste of the tropics to your dessert table. Its moist crumb and sweet, fruity flavor make it a refreshing and enjoyable cake for any occasion!

Cocoa Cake

Ingredients:

For the Cake:

- 1 3/4 cups all-purpose flour
- 1 1/2 cups granulated sugar
- 3/4 cup unsweetened cocoa powder
- 1 1/2 tsp baking powder
- 1 1/2 tsp baking soda
- 1/2 tsp salt
- 2 large eggs
- 1 cup milk (whole or 2%)
- 1/2 cup vegetable oil
- 2 tsp vanilla extract
- 1 cup boiling water

For the Chocolate Frosting (Optional):

- 1 cup unsalted butter, room temperature
- 3-4 cups powdered sugar
- 1/2 cup unsweetened cocoa powder
- 1/4 cup milk (or more, as needed)
- 1 tsp vanilla extract

Optional Garnish:

- Chocolate shavings
- Sprinkles
- Fresh berries

Instructions:

1. **Preheat Oven:**
   - Preheat your oven to 350°F (175°C). Grease and flour two 8-inch round cake pans or line them with parchment paper.
2. **Prepare the Cake Batter:**
   - In a large bowl, sift together the flour, granulated sugar, cocoa powder, baking powder, baking soda, and salt.
   - In another bowl, whisk together the eggs, milk, vegetable oil, and vanilla extract.
   - Gradually add the wet ingredients to the dry ingredients, mixing until just combined.
   - Stir in the boiling water. The batter will be thin, but this is normal.
3. **Bake the Cake:**
   - Divide the batter evenly between the prepared cake pans.

- Bake for 30-35 minutes, or until a toothpick inserted into the center comes out clean.
- Allow the cakes to cool in the pans for 10 minutes before transferring them to a wire rack to cool completely.

4. **Prepare the Chocolate Frosting (Optional):**
   - In a large bowl, beat the butter until creamy and smooth.
   - Gradually add the powdered sugar and cocoa powder, beating until combined and fluffy.
   - Mix in the milk, one tablespoon at a time, until you reach your desired consistency.
   - Add the vanilla extract and beat until well combined.

5. **Assemble and Frost the Cake:**
   - Once the cakes are completely cooled, spread a layer of frosting on top of one cake layer.
   - Place the second cake layer on top and frost the top and sides of the cake with the remaining frosting.

6. **Garnish and Serve:**
   - Garnish with chocolate shavings, sprinkles, or fresh berries if desired.
   - Slice and enjoy your Cocoa Cake!

Tips:

- **Cocoa Powder:** Use high-quality unsweetened cocoa powder for the best flavor. Dutch-process cocoa can be used for a smoother flavor.
- **Boiling Water:** Adding boiling water to the batter helps to dissolve the cocoa powder and creates a very moist cake.
- **Texture:** If you prefer a denser cake, reduce the amount of boiling water slightly. For a lighter cake, use the full amount.

Cocoa Cake is a classic favorite that's rich and chocolatey, perfect for any chocolate lover. Whether enjoyed plain or with a decadent frosting, it's a delicious treat that's sure to satisfy your sweet tooth!

Grape Cake

Ingredients:

For the Cake:

- 2 cups seedless grapes (fresh or frozen)
- 1 1/2 cups all-purpose flour
- 1 cup granulated sugar
- 1/2 cup unsalted butter, room temperature
- 2 large eggs
- 1/2 cup milk (whole or 2%)
- 1 1/2 tsp baking powder
- 1/2 tsp baking soda
- 1/4 tsp salt
- 1 tsp vanilla extract
- 1/2 tsp lemon zest (optional, for added freshness)

For the Glaze (Optional):

- 1/4 cup grape juice or white wine
- 1/4 cup granulated sugar
- 1 tsp cornstarch

For Garnish (Optional):

- Fresh grape slices
- Powdered sugar

Instructions:

1. **Prepare the Grapes:**
   - If using fresh grapes, wash them thoroughly and cut them in half. If using frozen grapes, thaw and drain them well to remove excess moisture.
2. **Preheat Oven:**
   - Preheat your oven to 350°F (175°C). Grease and flour a 9-inch round cake pan or line it with parchment paper.
3. **Prepare the Cake Batter:**
   - In a medium bowl, whisk together the flour, baking powder, baking soda, and salt.
   - In a large bowl, cream together the butter and granulated sugar until light and fluffy.
   - Add the eggs one at a time, beating well after each addition.
   - Mix in the vanilla extract and lemon zest (if using).
   - Gradually add the dry ingredients to the butter mixture, alternating with the milk. Begin and end with the dry ingredients, mixing until just combined.
   - Fold in the grape halves gently.

4. **Bake the Cake:**
   - Pour the batter into the prepared cake pan and smooth the top.
   - Bake for 35-40 minutes, or until a toothpick inserted into the center comes out clean.
   - Allow the cake to cool in the pan for 10 minutes before transferring it to a wire rack to cool completely.
5. **Prepare the Glaze (Optional):**
   - In a small saucepan, combine the grape juice (or white wine) and granulated sugar.
   - Stir in the cornstarch and heat over medium heat, stirring constantly until the mixture thickens and becomes clear.
   - Brush the glaze over the cooled cake for a shiny finish.
6. **Garnish and Serve:**
   - Garnish with fresh grape slices and a dusting of powdered sugar if desired.
   - Slice and enjoy your Grape Cake!

Tips:

- **Grapes:** Ensure the grapes are well-drained if using frozen grapes to avoid excess moisture in the batter.
- **Texture:** For a more even distribution of grapes, lightly coat them in flour before folding them into the batter.
- **Storage:** Store the cake in an airtight container at room temperature for up to 3 days, or refrigerate for longer shelf life.

Grape Cake is a delightful dessert that offers a refreshing twist with the inclusion of grapes. Whether enjoyed with or without glaze, it's a delicious way to savor the flavors of fresh fruit in a baked treat.

Mochi Cake

Ingredients:

- 1 1/2 cups glutinous rice flour (sweet rice flour)
- 1 cup granulated sugar
- 1/2 tsp baking powder
- 1/4 tsp salt
- 1 cup coconut milk (or whole milk)
- 3 large eggs
- 1/4 cup unsalted butter, melted
- 1 tsp vanilla extract (optional)
- 1/4 cup shredded coconut (optional)

Instructions:

1. **Preheat Oven:**
   - Preheat your oven to 350°F (175°C). Grease and flour an 8-inch square baking pan or line it with parchment paper.
2. **Prepare the Batter:**
   - In a large bowl, whisk together the glutinous rice flour, granulated sugar, baking powder, and salt.
   - In another bowl, whisk together the coconut milk, eggs, melted butter, and vanilla extract (if using).
   - Gradually add the wet ingredients to the dry ingredients, mixing until smooth and well combined.
   - If using, fold in the shredded coconut.
3. **Bake the Cake:**
   - Pour the batter into the prepared baking pan and smooth the top.
   - Bake for 30-35 minutes, or until the cake is set and a toothpick inserted into the center comes out clean.
   - The top should be lightly golden brown.
4. **Cool and Serve:**
   - Allow the cake to cool in the pan for about 10 minutes before transferring it to a wire rack to cool completely.
   - Cut into squares or rectangles and serve.

Tips:

- **Texture:** Mochi Cake has a dense and chewy texture. If you prefer a softer texture, you can slightly reduce the baking time.
- **Flavors:** You can experiment with different flavorings by adding ingredients like matcha powder, cocoa powder, or fruit extracts.
- **Storage:** Store the cake in an airtight container at room temperature for up to 3 days. It can also be refrigerated for up to a week or frozen for longer storage.

Mochi Cake is a delightful treat that combines the chewy texture of mochi with the rich flavor of a cake. Whether enjoyed plain or with added flavors, it's a unique and satisfying dessert that's sure to please!

Sorghum Cake

Ingredients:

For the Cake:

- 1 1/2 cups sorghum flour
- 1/2 cup all-purpose flour (or more sorghum flour for a gluten-free version)
- 1 cup granulated sugar
- 1/2 cup unsalted butter, room temperature
- 2 large eggs
- 1/2 cup milk (or dairy-free milk)
- 1/4 cup honey or molasses
- 1 1/2 tsp baking powder
- 1/2 tsp baking soda
- 1/4 tsp salt
- 1 tsp vanilla extract
- 1/2 tsp ground cinnamon (optional)
- 1/4 tsp ground ginger (optional)

For the Glaze (Optional):

- 1/2 cup powdered sugar
- 1-2 tbsp milk or water
- 1/2 tsp vanilla extract

For Garnish (Optional):

- Fresh fruit
- Nuts
- Powdered sugar

Instructions:

1. **Preheat Oven:**
   - Preheat your oven to 350°F (175°C). Grease and flour an 8-inch round cake pan or line it with parchment paper.
2. **Prepare the Batter:**
   - In a medium bowl, whisk together the sorghum flour, all-purpose flour (if using), baking powder, baking soda, salt, and optional spices (cinnamon and ginger).
   - In a large bowl, cream together the butter and granulated sugar until light and fluffy.
   - Add the eggs one at a time, beating well after each addition.
   - Mix in the vanilla extract and honey or molasses.
   - Gradually add the dry ingredients to the butter mixture, alternating with the milk, beginning and ending with the dry ingredients. Mix until just combined.

3. **Bake the Cake:**
   - Pour the batter into the prepared cake pan and smooth the top.
   - Bake for 25-30 minutes, or until a toothpick inserted into the center comes out clean.
   - Allow the cake to cool in the pan for 10 minutes before transferring it to a wire rack to cool completely.
4. **Prepare the Glaze (Optional):**
   - In a small bowl, whisk together the powdered sugar, milk (or water), and vanilla extract until smooth.
   - Drizzle over the cooled cake.
5. **Garnish and Serve:**
   - Garnish with fresh fruit, nuts, or a dusting of powdered sugar if desired.
   - Slice and enjoy your Sorghum Cake!

Tips:

- **Texture:** Sorghum flour can create a denser cake compared to all-purpose flour. If you prefer a lighter texture, consider using a blend of sorghum and all-purpose flour.
- **Sweeteners:** Adjust the sweetness by using more or less honey or molasses to suit your taste.
- **Flavor Variations:** Experiment with additional flavorings like citrus zest or spices to customize the cake to your preference.

Sorghum Cake offers a unique flavor profile and is a great way to incorporate sorghum flour into your baking. Enjoy its rich, nutty taste and chewy texture!

Chestnut and Red Bean Cake

Ingredients:

For the Cake:

- 1 cup chestnut puree (from canned chestnuts or homemade)
- 1 cup red bean paste (sweetened, store-bought or homemade)
- 1 cup all-purpose flour
- 1/2 cup granulated sugar
- 1/2 cup unsalted butter, room temperature
- 2 large eggs
- 1/2 cup milk (whole or 2%)
- 1 1/2 tsp baking powder
- 1/4 tsp salt
- 1 tsp vanilla extract

For the Glaze (Optional):

- 1/4 cup apricot jam or honey
- 1 tbsp water

For Garnish (Optional):

- Toasted chestnut pieces
- Red bean paste (for decoration)

Instructions:

1. **Preheat Oven:**
    - Preheat your oven to 350°F (175°C). Grease and flour an 8-inch round cake pan or line it with parchment paper.
2. **Prepare the Batter:**
    - In a medium bowl, whisk together the flour, baking powder, and salt.
    - In a large bowl, cream together the butter and granulated sugar until light and fluffy.
    - Add the eggs one at a time, beating well after each addition.
    - Mix in the chestnut puree and vanilla extract until well combined.
    - Gradually add the dry ingredients to the butter mixture, alternating with the milk. Begin and end with the dry ingredients, mixing until just combined.
    - Fold in the red bean paste gently.
3. **Bake the Cake:**
    - Pour the batter into the prepared cake pan and smooth the top.
    - Bake for 30-35 minutes, or until a toothpick inserted into the center comes out clean.

          - Allow the cake to cool in the pan for 10 minutes before transferring it to a wire rack to cool completely.
    4. **Prepare the Glaze (Optional):**
          - In a small saucepan, combine the apricot jam (or honey) and water.
          - Heat over low heat, stirring until the mixture is smooth and slightly thin.
          - Brush the glaze over the cooled cake for a shiny finish.
    5. **Garnish and Serve:**
          - Garnish with toasted chestnut pieces and a dollop of red bean paste if desired.
          - Slice and enjoy your Chestnut and Red Bean Cake!

Tips:

- **Chestnut Puree:** If using canned chestnuts, drain them and blend until smooth. If making homemade chestnut puree, roast and peel the chestnuts before blending.
- **Red Bean Paste:** Ensure the red bean paste is sweetened to your taste. Adjust the amount if needed.
- **Texture:** For a smoother texture, you can sift the flour before mixing it into the batter.

Chestnut and Red Bean Cake is a unique and flavorful dessert that combines two classic ingredients in a delightful way. Enjoy the rich taste and chewy texture of this special cake!

www.ingramcontent.com/pod-product-compliance
Lightning Source LLC
LaVergne TN
LVHW081558060526
838201LV00054B/1962